Praise for the Community College Transfer Guide

"The *Community College Transfer Guide* is a must read for students. I highly recommend that community college instructors adopt this book for College 101 or College Orientation courses. This book is also a useful tool for community college transfer advisors to use in their work with transfer students."
— Frankie Santos Laanan, Ph.D.
    Director, Office of Community College Research and Policy
    Associate Professor, Higher Education Program Coordinator
    Iowa State University

"The *Community College Transfer Guide* is comprehensive in providing information for students, parents, counselors and advisors. The Guide is easy to understand and covers all the bases on how to transfer from a community college to a four-year college or university. It's very helpful for counselors and advisors for themselves and when working with students one-on-one or as a text for transfer workshops and orientation classes. And it's inexpensive and well worth the money — a real key in this day and age."
— Martha M. Ellis, Ph.D., Associate Vice Chancellor for Community College
    Partnerships, *University of Texas System*

"*Community College Transfer Guide* provides transfer students with a wealth of resources, advice, and information. It has short, easy-to-read chapters. It is a comprehensive workbook that incorporates charts, checklists, and practical advice to make the complex transfer issue *user-friendly* to students, advisors, and faculty. Readers will benefit from subjects such as articulated courses as opposed to transferable classes, articulation agreements, and guaranteed admissions."
— *National Academic Advising Association* (NACADA *Journal*)

"The *Community College Transfer Guide* is an excellent resource for transfer workshops."
— Deborah Guy, Academic Advisor, *Palm Beach Community College*

"I have found the book to be extremely helpful. It is a practical guide to all the two-year transfer issues. I use it as a reference and in presentations. I would definitely recommend it to others."
— Dr. Brian Meredith, Director of Admissions, *University of Memphis*

"The *Community College Transfer Guide* is not only valuable to students, it offers relevant suggestions for transfer counselors as they organize and provide transfer advice."
— Daniel de la Torre, M.Ed., Coordinator of Transfer/Articulation
   Quinsigamond Community College

"*Community College Transfer Guide* is a comprehensive resource that can serve as a powerful guide for students seeking to navigate the transfer process."
— George Niebling, Strategic Initiatives Director, *University of North Texas* and
   the *National Institute for the Study of Transfer Students*

"The *Community College Transfer Guide* provides an abundance of knowledge to help students ease into University life."
— Rebecca A. Egbert, Senior Assistant Director of Admissions, Office of
   Undergraduate Admissions, *The University of North Carolina at Chapel Hill*

"The *Community College Transfer Guide* should be strongly considered by those in community college."
— *Midwest Book Review*

"This guide offers the student and for that matter the counselor a valuable tool...very thorough and comprehensive...The essentials are all here and easy to utilize."
— *The California School Counselor*

"Great, very comprehensive!"
— Bruce Vancil, Assistant Director of Transfer and Reentry Services
   California State University, Long Beach

"The *Community College Transfer Guide* leaves no stone unturned."
— Yoly Woo-Hoogenstyn, UCSD alum and former transfer student who
   currently works professionally in the transfer field

"Successful transfer from community college to a four-year college requires advance planning and the *Community College Transfer Guide* is an excellent resource to help students with every part of the transfer process. The checklists sections will keep students on track to make their transfer goals a reality."
— Martha "Marty" O'Connell, Executive Director, *Colleges That Change Lives*

Community College Transfer Guide

Don Silver

Adams-Hall Publishing
Los Angeles
www.adams-hall.com

Library of Congress Cataloging-in-Publication Data

Silver, Don
  Community College Transfer Guide/ Don Silver.
    p. cm.
  ISBN-13: 978-0-944708-84-2
1. Students, Transfer of—United States—Handbooks, manuals, etc. 2. Transfer students—United States—Handbooks, manuals, etc. 3. Community college students—United States—Transfer. I. Title.
  LB2360.S53 2009
  418.0071—dc22
            2009004436

Adams-Hall books are available at special, quantity discounts for bulk purchases, sales promotions, premiums, fundraising or educational use. For details, contact Adams-Hall Publishing at **800.888.4452** or **info@adams-hall.com**.

Printed in the United States of America
10 9 8 7 6 5 4 3 2

Acknowledgments

Transferring from a community college to a four-year college or university can be a very complex process. This book was written to not only provide a pathway to make your transition successful but also to point out and help you avoid what can go wrong along the way. To that end I am very grateful to Emily Forrest Cataldi, Daniel L. Nannini, Bruce Vancil and Yoly Woo-Hoogenstyn for their invaluable suggestions. I also want to thank Ralph Marks for his expert editing. In the end, however, I am responsible for all of the content as the author. It is my hope and goal that by reading this book, you will save time and money in attaining your bachelor's degree.

Also by Don Silver

High School Money Book
A Parent's Guide to Wills & Trusts
Teach Your Computer to Dance
Baby Boomer Retirement
Cookin' the Book$

Table of Contents

Table of Charts/Checklists

Chapter 1
Why You Need This Guide

It is a lot more complex transferring from a community college to a four-year college (or university) than it is going directly from high school.

Why is that? High schools have established, uniform college preparation coursework that can be used to apply to almost any college. By contrast, there is *no* universal transfer admission policy to get you or the six million other community college students into a four-year college or university.

Bottom line, to get where you want to go, you'll need to plan and navigate your way through a maze of transfer requirements and application procedures. The key is to have the right information and a transfer plan that will keep you on course. That's why you need this guide. Or else, as Hall of Fame catcher Yogi Berra once said, "If you don't know where you're going, you'll end up someplace else."

Note: In this guide the phrase "four-year college" will refer to both four-year colleges *and* four-year universities and "counselor" will refer to both advisors and counselors. Also, some topics in this guide are covered in more than one place if they're especially important or the context merits a reminder about them. Finally, there's a glossary at the end if you need to look up any of the terms used in this guide and a complete index for later reference.

Before getting into the how-to details on transferring, read Chapter 2 to see why it makes a lot of dollars and sense for you to get your bachelor's degree at a four-year college after first attending community college.

Chapter 2
How Community College and a Bachelor's Degree Will Benefit You

Community college benefits

You've made a smart move going to a community college. This way you have a college that:

- may give you *priority for admission* or may even *guarantee your admission* (see Chapter 10) at a public four-year college as a transfer student coming from an in-state community college
- is inexpensive
- opens admission to almost anyone
- allows you to make up (or overcome) any deficiencies in high school classes and grades
- offers smaller class sizes
- is in locations all across the U.S., making it more accessible (and also easier to live at home and save money)
- allows part-time or full-time enrollment, making it easier to accommodate flexible work and education schedules (more than 60% of community college students attend part-time but research shows that full-time students are more likely to transfer)
- provides a college experience and training ground before you move on to a four-year college

How much does it pay to have a four-year college degree?

Why should you bother to transfer to a four-year college and get a bachelor's degree? Currently, there are two financial benefits of having a four-year college degree.

First, the average yearly income for college graduates with a bachelor's degree is 50% higher than the yearly income of high school graduates.

Second, having a college degree gives you a greater choice in the work world (and maybe the romantic world) for your entire life. In other words, you become more desirable.

Of course, not everyone needs a college degree to be successful in life or successful financially. But whatever path your life takes, having a bachelor's degree helps put the odds in your favor and gives you more choices and opportunities.

Dollars and sense

And to keep your options open after college, keep in mind that finding the right four-year college does involve dollars and *sense*—you don't want to have too much debt (in college loans) when you leave college. That's probably part of the reason why you're going to community college—you can get a high quality education for a fraction of the cost (see Chapter 9).

The payoff for you

So how can college benefit you? College means more than increasing your earning power. It's also a way to develop interests, interpersonal skills and relationships that may benefit you the rest of your life.

As you try hard to do well in your classes and work through the transfer steps, keep these financial and non-financial benefits in mind whenever you need encouragement and assurance that the effort is worth it.

To maximize your payoff, you'll want to plan your transfer as early as possible. Chapter 3 tells you why early planning is so important.

Chapter 3

Why You Need to Do Transfer Planning As Early As Possible

When it comes to transferring, what you don't know *can* hurt you.

Without advance planning, you may find out too late that you've been taking courses at community college that:

- won't transfer to any four-year college
- won't fulfill admission or graduation requirements at a particular four-year college of your choice
- won't get you admitted to your major in a particular four-year college
- won't get you admitted to a four-year college *when* you expect or
- won't leave you enough financial aid because you used up your benefits taking the wrong courses

Without advance planning, it could take much longer to graduate. In fact, only about one-third of students complete a bachelor's degree as soon as four years after entering college and it is not unusual for students to take five, six or more years to graduate. In general, the more colleges a student attends, the longer it takes to graduate. Since you don't want extra unnecessary delays and expenses, you need to get the right transfer information as soon as possible and have a transfer plan.

With advance planning, you'll be better prepared to find the right four-year colleges for you and to take advantage of transfer opportunities as soon as possible. Taking the wrong courses can delay your progress. The earlier you start planning, the more time you'll have to: determine your career and life goals, find a major that fulfills those goals, select the right four-year colleges that will help you achieve your dreams, take the right courses to enhance your chances of being admitted to the four-year colleges of your choice and use your financial aid wisely.

Knowing the right courses to take at community college will save you time, money and aggravation. So will knowing the pre-transfer issues covered in Chapter 4.

Chapter 4
Important Pre-Transfer Issues

Before you dig into the detailed transfer planning process, take a few moments to read about some big picture pre-transfer issues that are important for you.

Choose the right community college

Planning starts with finding the right community college. Some community colleges are more successful than others at having students transfer to four-year colleges. Some community colleges may also have a stronger transfer relationship with particular four-year colleges. If you have a choice, you may want to select one of these community colleges over another for these reasons.

Look at state websites (e.g., in California, see *www.cccapply.org/Select/*) to compare community colleges, see key facts and help determine which community college best meets your requirements.

See whether a four-year college accepts transfer students

Most, but not all, four-year colleges take transfer students. Some four-year colleges are more interested than others in having transfer students. Some four-year colleges give priority to students in community colleges in their area or in their state.

Find out if there's a guaranteed admission program to four-year colleges

Chapter 10 has more details on how some community colleges have guaranteed admission programs with particular four-year colleges.

Decide whether to transfer to a four-year college as a sophomore or a junior

When you want to transfer not only affects money issues but also admission requirements. Generally, you'll be transferring as a sophomore or a junior. Some four-year colleges accept freshman transfers. (See Chapter 12 regarding issues and potential obstacles on transferring if you have too many units.)

Transferring as a sophomore

If you want to transfer as a sophomore, your high school transcript and SAT/ACT scores may be more important factors unless you've already completed a specified number of transferable community college units by the time you apply (often 30 semester units — it depends on the requirements of each four-year college).

Transferring as a junior

If you want to transfer as a junior, chances are your community college grades will be extremely important and your SAT/ACT scores and high school grades may be of lesser or no importance — it depends on the admission criteria of each four-year college. There's no one policy for all four-year colleges.

And if your earlier academic performance in high school wasn't as good as your community college grades, you may decide to wait to apply as a junior transfer so you'll have a better academic record. (Some four-year colleges only accept transfers for the junior year anyway.)

Transferring as a junior will also save you money on college tuition costs.

Select a major and plan accordingly

The major you select will affect not only the lower-division courses in your major you may need to take at community college but also possibly the General Education courses, too. The reason is that once you select a major and identify possible four-year colleges offering that major, the General Education and lower-division major coursework needed to get admitted into *each* four-year college may vary.

Plan your coursework to maximize your transfer possibilities by having most or all of the community college courses you take meet the requirements for *several* four-year colleges.

Plan more carefully if you want to transfer to an out-of-state or private college

Often, the easiest way to transfer is from a community college in your state to a four-year public college in the *same state*.

That means if you plan to transfer to a four-year college in another state or to a private institution in or out of the state where your community college is located, it is often more difficult to determine which of your community college courses will be accepted when you transfer. Contact the four-year colleges you're considering as early as possible to determine how your community college coursework will be evaluated.

Keep on planning and getting counseling

Since four-year college programs, majors and entrance requirements can change *at any time*, it's a good idea to follow the steps described in this guide not just once but every semester you're in community college. Each semester be sure to meet with your community college counselor and to contact the admissions department at the four-year colleges you're considering to review the current requirements. For information on courses that will satisfy major requirements, sometimes talking directly with the department of your major at the four-year college can be very useful.

Be aware that some four-year college admissions departments will require that you apply first before they'll provide information on the transferability of the actual courses you've taken or the ones you're thinking of taking.

Get a two-year community college Associate degree

Don't just plan to transfer. See if you can also get a two-year degree at the same time from your community college. Most common is the Associate of Arts (A.A.) degree but also available at most colleges are the Associate of Science (A.S.) and Associate of Business (A.B.) degrees. Here's the advantage: if circumstances prevent or delay you from getting a bachelor's degree, you will always have your Associate degree as an accomplishment. Another benefit of an Associate degree is that some state programs (see Chapter 10) guarantee your admission to a public four-year college in the same state if you have an A.A. degree. (Note, however, that you may not be guaranteed admission to a particular major unless you meet other requirements.)

Have a Plan B

You may not get into the four-year college or major of your dreams—that's your Plan A. That's why you want to have a Plan B and apply to probably at least six four-year colleges.

Some final thoughts

As you go through the application process, remember this: You may not get into your "perfect" college but a rejection by a college is *not* a measure of your self-worth and for every door that closes in life, another one opens.

Going to a particular college does not guarantee success in life, nor does it prevent it.

Above all, you need to be a *great person* in life more than you need to graduate from a *great college*.

But since your goal is to become a transfer student, read Chapter 5 so you'll understand what is meant by "transfer credits" and other jargon you need to know.

Chapter 5
Transfer Credit Jargon You Need to Know

There's a special lingo (language) when it comes to college credits. Credits are sometimes called *units* or *hours*. It's important for you to understand what the various words mean since they can affect:

- whether you get into the four-year college or major of your choice and/or
- how long it will take you to graduate with a bachelor's degree

To get the most out of your community college courses, you need to understand five types of *transfer credits* and also the difference between *transferable courses* and *articulated courses*. In this chapter you'll learn about the five types of college transfer credits and then, in Chapter 14, you'll learn the difference between transferable courses and articulated courses—a very important factor for determining which community college courses you should take.

Five Types of College Transfer Credits

Just as it's important to understand and protect your credit in the money world, it's essential to maximize your credits in the college world.

Four-year colleges may count your community college course units in up to five different ways including:

1. General Education (GE) credit

Four-year colleges require you to take some General Education (GE) courses in English, math, arts, humanities, social and behavioral sciences and physical and biological sciences before or possibly after entering the four-year college. These GE requirements vary from school to school.

2. Lower-division major course credit

You can get credit for lower-division courses in your major (typically taken during freshman and sophomore years) that a four-year college wants or even *requires* you to take at community college before being admitted to the major. These courses may also give you credit for General Education requirements, too.

3. Elective credit

Elective units count toward graduation at a four-year college but are *not* counted as GE or lower-division major course units. This type of credit is not as useful as GE or lower-division major credits since these units do not fulfill a course requirement. Since four-year colleges have limits on how many overall units *can* be transferred, there is a risk that elective courses may not count at all if the overall unit limit is exceeded. Use your elective credits wisely.

4. Credit for the application process vs. actual graduation credit

Four-year colleges usually require transfer students to have taken a minimum number of transferable units at community college before applying to transfer. But what counts at one four-year college may not count at another. That's why you have to check out the individual requirements at *each* four-year college you're interested in.

And just because a four-year college gives you course credits towards the minimum *application requirements* does not necessarily mean that the college will count those same units towards *graduation requirements*. For example, UCLA counts four *semester* units of physical education courses for admission purposes but only counts four *quarter* units towards graduation. So before you agree to attend any given four-year college, ask for a *transfer credit report* to know how many of your community college credits will actually count as General Education, lower-division major coursework and elective credit for graduation purposes.

5. For no credit at all

Getting no credit at all is the worst result for you. But don't worry. Most if not all of your community college courses will probably count toward graduation at a four-year college. However, you *may* not get credit for some or all of the following: vocational courses, remedial courses, credits that are too old (if you've been out of school for quite a while and the subject matter of a course has changed over time, some four-year colleges won't give credit for the course) or courses from unaccredited schools. Check with community college and four-year college counselors for more information on your particular courses.

Now that you understand the five types of transfer credits, it's time to learn in Chapter 6 the secrets to transferring successfully.

Chapter 6
Secrets to Transferring Successfully

You can make your transfer process smoother and more successful if you:

- choose a major as soon as possible that meets your educational, work, career and life goals

- select the right four-year colleges for you that offer that major

- research the admission, transfer and graduation requirements for those four-year colleges including guaranteed admission programs (covered in Chapters 10 and 12)

- meet with a community college counselor *every semester before registering for courses* to discuss your major, the four-year colleges you have in mind and the community college coursework you need to take to transfer successfully

- meet or talk with representatives of your top four-year college choices

- know the difference between articulated courses and transferable courses (covered in Chapter 14)

- select the General Education *and* lower-division major courses at community college that minimize the time it takes to transfer your articulated and transferable units *and* maximize your chances for admission in your major at the college of your choice

If you think that you only need to take General Education (GE) courses at community college to transfer to a four-year college, you may be in for a big surprise.

When transferring very often it is *more important* to take lower-division courses in your major at community college than it is to take *all* your GE courses. This is especially true for majors (such as those in engineering and biology) that require extensive preparation during the lower-division years at community college.

Ideally, you'll take both lower-division courses in your major *and* GE courses at community college. How important is it to take courses at community college in your major as compared to GE courses? The answer is that it depends on the requirements for your major at the four-year colleges you want to attend.

Here's where it can get more complicated. The same major at two different four-year colleges may require different courses for admission. Different majors at the same four-year college may require different courses for admission.

That's why advance planning is so important. Try to use the same courses to meet the requirements of as many of your four-year college choices as possible. For example, you may have to take a course to meet a General Education humanities requirement. Each four-year college you're interested in may only accept a different humanities course except for one course that will be accepted at all of them. You can save time and money by taking that one commonly required course. Here are more secrets:

- complete all of your General Education courses at community college and you will graduate sooner

- develop a working relationship with your community college professors and counselors and stay in contact with them so they'll know you well enough to give you a letter of recommendation either for admission or scholarships when you apply to four-year colleges

- maintain a word processing file (and printout) of the catalog descriptions of all of the community college courses you've taken (organized by semester and year) and at a minimum, retain syllabi from your courses — you might also want to retain, in organized folders, the papers you've written for each course and any tests you've received back

You'll want to keep this information in case a four-year college denies credit for a course you've taken. Four-year colleges set their own requirements for determining whether a course is sufficiently challenging or consistent with their curriculum. You may be able to overcome a denial of transferability by providing sufficient information on a course (e.g., catalog course descriptions, syllabi, etc.). If you update and organize this information each semester as you go through community college, you'll be in a good position to easily send additional information to justify why a course should receive credit if the need arises.

Each course that you can change from a non-transferable course to a transferable course could save you thousands of dollars in tuition at a four-year college.

- join an academic honor society while in community college (e.g., Phi Theta Kappa at *www.ptk.org*) through a local chapter at your college if you have good grades so you'll not only have another honor to add to your transfer application but also possibly be eligible for a special scholarship (e.g., Phi Theta Kappa) when you transfer to a four-year college

- handle college, housing and financial aid applications in a timely and complete manner

Now you're ready for the 10 key steps in transferring.

Chapter 7
The 10 Key Steps in Transferring

The transfer process is like putting a puzzle together. The pieces have to fit together just right. Each of the 10 puzzle pieces listed below represents a key step in the transfer process. The first step is most important, however, because it can affect every other part of the transfer process.

The 10 Key Steps

Take these steps as soon as possible (with the help of your community college counselor):

Step #1:   Select the right major *for you* (Chapter 8).

Step #2:   Understand money and the other big issues *before* you start looking for a four-year college (Chapter 9; also see Chapter 6).

Step #3:   See if there are transfer guarantee programs where four-year colleges guarantee your admission (Chapter 10).

Step #4:   Assemble a list of the four-year colleges you should investigate (Chapter 11).

Step #5:   Research the admission, transfer *and* graduation requirements for those four-year colleges (Chapter 12).

Step #6:   Ask the key questions about each four-year college you want to attend (Chapter 13).

Step #7:   Find the right courses you need to take at community college to transfer to each of these four-year colleges (Chapter 14).

Step #8:   Find the money needed to attend these four-year colleges (Chapter 15).

Step #9:   Visit the campuses (Chapter 16).

Step #10:   Complete the transfer applications (Chapter 17).

The remainder of this guide contains information pertinent to each of these steps and is designed to facilitate and simplify your transfer process.

Chapter 8

Step #1: Select the Right Major For You

Although *some* four-year colleges allow you to transfer as an *undecided* (without a major), you'll want to select a major as soon as possible. That will help you determine which courses you need to take at community college to transfer to the four-year colleges of your choice.

Finding the right major is similar to the personal process of buying shoes. You need to find the right size and fit for you. Just as a shoe may look great but not be the right fit, deciding on the right major *for you* is very much a personal process.

If you haven't already decided on a major or you want to confirm that you've made the right choice, keep on reading. Even if you already know what your major will be, it will be worthwhile for you to read this chapter.

You may think that the choice of a major is not as critical for you because your goal is just to get a bachelor's degree in any field at a particular four-year college (maybe a public four-year college to save on tuition money). But if you're like most students, you may find that selecting the right major will affect at least your initial career and life decisions.

Take General Education courses if you're still undecided

If, after reading this chapter, you are still undecided about your major but you know that you will eventually be transferring to a four-year college to pursue a bachelor's degree, it is probably best to keep taking General Education courses.

The subject matter of General Education courses or the enthusiasm and talents of a professor may spark your interest level toward a particular field and major.

In any event, it's not just the courses in your major that will be important to you later in life. Don't discount the value of liberal arts courses outside of your major. Although a specialized degree can help you get a job in a particular field, during your lifetime you may have seven to 20 different jobs and possibly five to 10 careers — not necessarily just in the field of your major.

Back in the early 1990s, very few people had any idea of the Internet's potential. What revolutionary changes will you see in the next 15 years? 30 years? Your keys to success will be enjoying your work (whatever it is), networking, enjoying being with family, friends and business colleagues, continuing to learn and grow and striving to be your best, whatever kind of work you do.

Determine your field of interest and career goal

Ideally, when you enter community college, start thinking about the kind of work you'll want to do after you complete college. Don't let the task overwhelm you since you will probably have many different kinds of jobs in several different fields over your work lifetime. However, you have to start somewhere.

If you have many different areas of interest, take a sheet of paper (or a computer screen) and label one half "pros" and the other "cons." Then, write down your top three areas of interest and list the pros and cons below them.

Factors to consider

Among the factors to consider for each area of interest are:

- your passion, skill and interest in the subject area

- how it will benefit society

- the likelihood of your being able to graduate in that field and find a job to your liking

- the amount of money and security a job in that field offers (and whether the college cost to enter that field is really worth it)

- whether you realistically have the skills to get through the required coursework as well as perform the actual work for the job. For example, it might sound nice to become a computer programmer but if you have no interest or talent for higher mathematics, the need to take several calculus courses might diminish your interest.

Job security

Here's a word about job security. The work world is constantly undergoing tremendous change. Some companies merge and come together, others reduce their workforce periodically to save money and some go bankrupt if they are unable to meet business challenges.

Your best job security is to always be learning and expanding your knowledge and skills. You may also have an entrepreneurial bent so your initial jobs may turn out to be learning experiences for the time you open your own business.

Since the best way to find a job is often through people you know, once you graduate be sure to continue to network with friends, business colleagues, college professors and fellow members of charitable and social organizations. Consider using social and professional networking sites to keep your name in front of people who may be hiring or know someone else who is hiring.

How to determine your field of interest

There are many ways to determine your main field of interest. One good way is to see it in action and to talk to people working in the field. For example, if you want to be a software programmer, call up software companies and make appointments to talk to or visit in person with programmers. Speak to people who have been working in the field two years, five years and ten years. See what their perspective is on the work, their enjoyment of it and whether they'd recommend that you enter the field in view of your interests and abilities and *their* experiences.

Then, every six months during your school years (and yearly throughout your work career), repeat this process of listing your career choices, writing down the pros and cons and conducting your real-world interviews.

Another good way to determine your field of interest is to get an internship or part-time job in your chosen field. Even if the work you're doing isn't at the level you hope to attain, you'll be able to observe the working conditions and attitudes of your fellow employees to see whether this is a career path you want to follow.

Get counseling

High school and community college counselors are invaluable sources who can not only give you advice on selecting a major but also the colleges for that major. See if your community college offers career assessments and career counseling. Career assessments can help you determine which major and/or career is the best match for you.

Research on the Net

There is a wide range of websites that can help you choose a major. Examples are shown below (brief descriptions are included for sites that aren't self-explanatory):

- *Choosing a Major*

  (*www.washington.edu/uaa/gateway/advising/majors/intro.php*)

- *What Can I Do With A Major In (www.uncwil.edu/stuaff/career/Majors/)*

- *What College Majors Will Match Your Personality?*
  (http://homeworktips.about.com/library/maj/bl_majors_quiz.htm)

- *Matching Majors to Occupations (www.career.fsu.edu/occupations/matchmajor/)*

- *Studentsreview.com*
  This website offers opinions from alumni and includes job satisfaction by major, salaries by major, whether alumni are still in the field of their major, a detailed description of what you learn in the major, what the fellow students are like and what kinds of jobs you generally get with it. *(www.studentsreview.com/choosing_career.php3)*

- *Occupational Outlook Handbook (www.bls.gov/oco/)*

  For hundreds of jobs, this online handbook tells you the training and education needed, earnings, expected job prospects, what workers do on the job and the working conditions. It also includes information about the job market in each state.

- *Career Guide to Industries (www.bls.gov/OCO/cg/)*

  This guide tells you about occupations in the industry, training and advancement, earnings, expected job prospects, working conditions and information on the job market in each state. It's a companion to the Occupational Outlook Handbook, which provides information on careers from an occupational perspective.

- *Career Information Net* on the U.S. Department of Labor website at *www.acinet.org/HelpAndInfo.asp?helpcontent=Students&nodeid=102*

- The O*NET system site *(http://online.onetcenter.org/)* provides comprehensive information on key attributes and characteristics of workers and occupations.

- *College Board Majors & Careers Central*

  www.collegeboard.com/student/csearch/majors_careers/index.html

- *Princeton Review Online*

  www.princetonreview.com/default.aspx?uidbadge=%07, click Careers & Majors; then click either Majors Search and/or More About Colleges & Majors

- *Choose Your Major and Campus* for the University of California

  http://uctransfer.universityofcalifornia.edu

Take a career development course

In a class you can learn how to match up your interests, talents and skills with different majors and careers.

Do a test run

Take a course in a major or a General Education subject to see whether you're interested in the field.

What if you change your major?

If you change your major once you're admitted to a four-year college, you will probably need to take other lower-division coursework in your major (e.g., switching from English to Computer Science will probably involve more math courses). Since changing your major may mean more time in college, you could run into time limits on your financial aid, depending on how long you'll be in college.

Once you've selected your major, you'll want to find the best colleges for you *that offer that major*. Before starting that process, make sure you understand money and other big issues in selecting a four-year college. That's the next step.

Chapter 9
Step #2: Understand Money and Other Big Issues

Once you decide on a major, you may have a handful of four-year colleges with the program you want to attend or a thousand to choose from. Before applying to any of them, here's a summary of key factors to consider.

Cost

Four-year *public colleges* are generally less expensive than four-year *private colleges*. *In-state* public colleges are generally less expensive than *out-of-state* public colleges.

Tuition reduction programs (which reduce or eliminate tuition depending on your family's income level) and financial aid may allow you to attend a more expensive college. There are two categories of financial aid — scholarships and grants, which you *don't* need to pay back, and loans, which you *do*.

Also see Chapter 15, *Find the Money to Attend a Four-Year College*.

College may be more affordable than you think. But figuring out in advance exactly how much *your* college education will cost isn't easy for three reasons:

1. *Sticker prices vs. net prices*

2. *Average net prices vs. your price*

3. *How long you'll be in college*

Sticker prices vs. net prices

If you walk into a car dealership to buy a car, you'll see a sticker price (cost) on a car's window or windshield. That's not the price you should pay for the car. Instead, through negotiation, you can get a lower price. Similarly, college tuition costs and fees have a sticker (published) price and a net price. Try not to pay the sticker price here either. Many students pay the sticker price because they are not aware of all the sources and amounts of grants and scholarships available to them that can reduce college costs.

Sticker prices

According to the College Board, for the 2009-2010 school year, the national average sticker (published) price for tuition and fees for one year of college was:

$2,544 at two-year public colleges

$7,020 at four-year public colleges and universities (for in-state residents)

$26,273 at four-year *private* colleges and universities

That's just one year's sticker price.

Net prices

Now look at the net prices. Here's the national average net price for tuition and fees for 2009-2010:

$0 (a $2,544 drop) at two-year public colleges

$1,600 (a $5,400 drop) at four-year public colleges and universities (for in-state residents)

$11,900 (a $14,400 drop) at four-year *private* colleges and universities

That's quite a difference. As you can see, going to a community college or a four-year public college or university can cut your costs considerably.

What are net prices? *Net prices* are the sticker prices *less* any grants, scholarships and higher education tax benefits (tax deductions and tax credits). Net prices show the true out-of-pocket costs.

Grants are financial aid, based on need, which you *don't* have to repay. Scholarships are given for all levels of profiles and talents (including special academic, artistic or athletic abilities) and *don't* need to be repaid. Scholarships can also be need-, merit- and affiliation-based. (Of course, loans, the other main type of financial aid, do need to be repaid.)

Average net prices vs. your price

Since average net prices vary by region, school and tax benefits, your cost might be very different. Also, it's difficult to predict your net price in advance because even within the same four-year college or university, students pay different net prices depending on their family income and resources, eligibility for grant aid, academic qualifications and other factors. However, average net prices and average sticker prices at least give you a range of dollar amounts that you can use as rough guidelines.

Other costs

Besides tuition and fees, books cost on average around $1,000 per year as do transportation costs. Room and board costs average around $7,500 per year (living at home can save money here).

How long you'll be in college

Yearly costs really add up so it's important to know for budgeting purposes when you'll graduate. Keep in mind that only 38% of students earn a bachelor's degree within four years of entering college. Extra years in college also mean extra time for education inflation to increase costs.

If you transfer to a four-year college as a junior, you can possibly graduate after just two years at a four-year school, shaving years off the average college stay.

That's why you really want to make your community college units count. You'll save time and big-time money at a four-year college if more of your community college units transfer and fulfill requirements. And with belt-tightening and cutbacks at four-year colleges becoming more common, it may be harder to find all the courses you'll need to graduate *when* you need to take them (and in the sequence you want). That could lengthen your stay (and cost) at a four-year college. So make the best use of your time at community college to minimize the time and money you'll spend at a four-year college.

Financial Aid

Most students or their families don't have savings to cover 100% of college costs. However, whatever can be saved will be a big help. In general, the difference between savings and costs can be paid through loans, grants, scholarships or other financial aid, including work-study programs. However, as time goes on, it's getting more difficult to find *enough* sources and *affordable* sources to pay all the college bills.

So you'll want to use *FAFSA4caster* (*www.fafsa4caster.ed.gov/*), a great tool from Federal Student Aid (*www.FederalStudentAid.ed.gov*), an office of the U.S. Department of Education. It provides you and your family with an early estimate of eligibility for federal student aid, the *Expected Family Contribution* (EFC) and eligibility for a Pell grant. The tool is based on the *FAFSA* (Free Application for Federal Student Aid), the qualifying form for federal financial aid. You can also do estimated aid calculations at *www.finaid.org/calculators/finaidestimate.phtml*.

FAFSA

Completing the *FAFSA* (Free Application for Federal Student Aid) is essential for getting financial aid.

In general, you can get the FAFSA forms in November of each year at *www.fafsa.ed.gov*. However, the earliest you can submit your information is on January 1 for the year you're trying for aid (e.g., to apply for aid for the 2010-2011 school year, you'd apply on or after January 1, 2010). Make sure you apply before your financial aid *priority deadline,* which can vary (e.g., February 15, March 2, etc.).

It's a good idea to start assembling the needed information in December. After you file the FAFSA, you'll receive (and so will the colleges you list on your FAFSA) a Student Aid Report from the federal government stating the expected family contribution for your college expenses. If there is a significant change of circumstances after you file the FAFSA (or a difference between estimated and actual filed income tax information), you can amend your FAFSA and also contact the colleges and universities that receive a copy of the report.

CSS PROFILE

You may also need to submit financial aid forms to four-year colleges and complete the College Scholarship Service (CSS)/Financial Aid Profile® (*https://profileonline.collegeboard.com/prf/index.jsp*), another financial aid form. Many four-year colleges use the financial information you provide on the CSS PROFILE to help them award non-federal student aid funds.

Deadlines for financial aid

There are federal deadlines, state deadlines and four-year college deadlines on financial aid that may or may not be the same as your four-year college application deadlines. Find out your priority deadline dates but don't wait until the deadline dates to apply for aid. Since financial aid may be given out on a first-come, first-served basis, it's a good idea to apply earlier rather than later. By the time the deadline arrives, all or most of the financial aid funds may have already been given out. If you miss a priority deadline to apply by one day, it may cost you 80% or more of the free grant money you would have received.

Staying qualified for next year's aid

To qualify for financial aid for the next school year, you may also need to take a specified number of units and maintain a specified minimum GPA.

Besides money, other important issues to consider are covered below.

Retention and graduation rates

A good way to know how satisfied students are with a four-year college is to see the retention rate (the percentage who return after their freshman year). You can get this information on the *College Navigator* website (go to *http://nces.ed.gov/collegenavigator/* and type in a college's name).

Another good way to measure the quality of a four-year college is the graduation rate (the percentage of entering students who stay to graduate) — you can also find this information on the *College Navigator* website. If a four-year college has good retention and graduation rates, it's an indicator that there are probably good academic, financial and social support systems in place to help students.

College ranking / quality of the faculty and students

You can get a good education at most colleges. Before putting too much weight on how a magazine or other publication ranks a four-year college, keep in mind that it might not be how you'd rank that college.

You can get a feel for a four-year college's quality by talking to professors, counselors and students. There are also websites and reference books on four-year colleges (see Chapter 11).

Admission requirements

Besides your community college coursework, find out whether you also need a minimum GPA; SAT/ACT scores; letters of recommendation; a portfolio; and a high school degree, GED (General Education Development) tests or a high school proficiency exam (e.g., CHSPE, the California High School Proficiency Exam) to be admitted.

Number of transfer credits you'll receive

Four-year colleges vary as to how much transfer credit you'll receive for your community college units. That affects how long you'll be attending a four-year college and how much your education will cost there.

Majors

Colleges vary in the majors they offer and the names they give the same major. If you have a specific major in mind, you may not find it at every college.

Colleges also vary in the internships they offer in their majors. Since real-world experience can help you decide whether to enter a field and also help you get a job once you graduate, see whether a strong internship program is important to you.

Location

You may want to live in another part of the country or experience a different environment whether it's the weather or an urban or rural setting. Remember that location can affect cost, too; if you're planning on living at home you could save money or if you'll be living away from home, you could have considerable living expenses.

Size

Larger colleges usually offer a broader range of majors. A potential downside of those colleges is larger class sizes. Although smaller four-year colleges usually give you more personal attention, you could be in a major in a small department at a large college.

Campus life and diversity

College is more than going to classes. The complete college experience includes social, athletic and extracurricular activities as well as academics. Find out what's available on campus and in the surrounding community to make your college experience more fulfilling.

You're in college to learn. You may learn more about the world by attending a diverse campus.

Housing

Housing is very important. In some cases, it can make or break the college experience. See if the off-campus housing is convenient and affordable and close enough to the four-year college so you'll feel part of the campus community. Also, find out whether you can get on-campus housing as a transfer student. Also see if there's a special dorm just for your major.

Colleges may have a first-come, first-served process to assign housing (as well as financial aid) so apply for housing as early as possible.

Support services

It may be very important for you to attend a four-year college that provides academic tutoring, career counseling and assessments, child care or support services for a physical disability.

Accreditation

You may get a bachelor's degree from an accredited four-year college or an unaccredited four-year college. *Regionally accredited* colleges are generally held to higher standards and are more prestigious. The difference could be very important as far as your getting a job with your degree. Check out the accreditation with your community college.

Adults returning to college

If you are an adult returning to college, you may need more help in locating the right college programs, financial aid and other needs. See the Back to College site (*www.back2college.com*) for more information.

Whatever your age, you may be able to participate in a guaranteed admission program. See Chapter 10 for details.

Chapter 10

Step #3: See If There Is a Guaranteed Admission Program

Some states have programs that guarantee admission to certain four-year colleges in those states if students:

- get an Associate degree (e.g., an A.A.) from a community college in that state and maintain a specified minimum GPA (grade point average) *or*

- sign a *transfer admission guarantee* (TAG) contract, complete the specified coursework at a community college in that state and maintain a specified minimum GPA (regardless of whether you get an Associate degree). Find out from your community college counselor which four-year colleges, if any, have a TAG and *when* you need to sign a TAG. TAGs go by different names such as *TAA (transfer admission agreement)* or *TAP (transfer advantage program)*.

- get admitted right out of high school to a *dual enrollment (co-admission)* program where one application process includes admission to both a community college and a four-year college

For example, with an A.A. degree from certain Florida community colleges, Florida's DirectConnect program gives you an admission guarantee to the University of Central Florida (*www.regionalcampuses.ucf.edu/directconnect.asp*).

For examples of TAG or TAP programs, see:

> California:
> *http://uctransfer.universityofcalifornia.edu/transfer_admis_guar.html*
>
> (you may also want to see the chart at
> *http://uctransfer.universityofcalifornia.edu/pdf/tag_matrix_and_form.pdf*)

Maryland:
www.uga.umd.edu/admissions/apply/MarylandTransferAdvantage.asp

With either the Associate degree or TAG/TAP method, find out whether you're also guaranteed admission to a particular major (probably not). To get the major you want, you still might need to take certain lower-division coursework in your major and meet other requirements.

For an example of a dual enrollment program, see the Oregon University system (*www.ous.edu/stucoun/campcent/dual.php*).

Combination of approaches

The California State University (CSU) system has TAG/TAA guarantees between certain CSU campuses and community colleges. It also has the *LDTP* (Lower Division Transfer Patterns) program with two components: (1) a statewide component giving students a road map for General Education *and* lower-division major courses that have statewide acceptance and (2) a campus component giving the highest priority for admission to a specific campus and major (subject to enrollment demand, available space and satisfactory completion of the requirements in the LDTP contract). See *www.calstate.edu/acadaff/ldtp* and *www.calstate.edu/acadaff/ldtp/docs/csu_ccc_mou.pdf*. Due to ongoing budget constraints, check with a CSU counselor as to whether the TAG/TAA and LDTP programs remain in effect for you.

Very important reminder—double-check

Whenever you see the word "guarantee," find out what it really means. *Double-check* with the four-year college(s) you have in mind. For example, in researching this book, I saw a transfer brochure on a community college site that said if a student completed a certain program, the student was "guaranteed admission" to the four-year colleges listed in the brochure. I contacted one of those four-year colleges and was told that there was *no guaranteed admission*, only a *guarantee of transferability of units* taken at the community college. I then contacted the community college and was told that the brochure on their website was *wrong* as far as *all* of the four-year colleges listed — only the *transferability of units* was guaranteed, *not admission*. Both the community college and the four-year college thanked me for pointing out this error and said the brochure would be corrected.

Even if you have a guaranteed acceptance program, you need to read Chapter 11.

Chapter 11

Step #4: Assemble a List of Four-Year Colleges to Investigate

Looking for colleges is like panning for gold. You sift through a lot of possibilities. If something doesn't pan out, you don't stop. You keep going until you find the gold you need. You'll probably want to apply to at least six four-year colleges. To save you time and aggravation, use the system described in Chapters 11 through 13 to find your college gold.

In Step #4 in this chapter, you're just coming up with an initial list of six possible four-year colleges to investigate further using Steps #5 and #6 (Chapters 12 and 13).

Be realistic

Be realistic as you go through these steps. Don't rule out a college too quickly. You may not find the "perfect" college. What you're looking for are four-year colleges that are a very good fit for you. Think about applying to your fallback choices, your realistic choices and your dream choices—you may want to apply to two or three colleges you feel you are sure to get into; three or four colleges where it is likely you'll get in; and two or three colleges you would really like to attend but where the odds are low that you'll get in.

Be organized

Keep an organized record on a computer file of all your college search efforts. Keep all the information you've found, even unlikely choices, readily available because what doesn't look great to you today may look a lot better after you compare it to the alternatives. You may end up applying to a four-year college you initially discarded. Also back up the information you find on an external drive as well as online (such as by an email to yourself with an attached file).

For this part of the search, just use a word processing file that includes the name of each four-year college you're considering, your thoughts on each college in one sentence and your numerical rating of the college from 1 to 10, with 10 being high.

How to assemble a list of four-year college possibilities

Assemble your list by doing as many of these steps as possible:

- talk to community college counselors and professors

- have conversations with people already working in the field you want to enter—get their opinions about which four-year colleges are the best (and why they're the best) for your getting hired when you graduate and reaching your career goal; also ask which colleges, if any, to avoid

- call the department at four-year colleges that offer the major you want and ask why a student would want to take courses in that major at that college as compared with other colleges (also ask how the department approaches the major—keep in mind that different colleges may have different approaches to the same major)

- read student reviews of four-year colleges on websites such as:

  www4.studentsreview.com (type in a name of a four-year college and then click on Student Surveys, Alumni Surveys or both)

  http://collegeprowler.com/ (then select a school)

  www.collegeconfidential.com

www.unigo.com

- talk to current students and alumni of four-year colleges as to what they like best about their four-year college and what could be improved (something can always be improved) — try to talk with people both in and outside your major

- talk to students who transferred from your community college to the four-year college

- see if your community college has *transfer guides* for specific four-year colleges

- find out the cost of tuition, fees, housing and meals and the availability of grants, scholarships, tuition reduction programs and any other financial aid

- go to transfer workshops (some workshops are college-specific while others are more general)

- attend college fairs

- visit college websites

- meet with representatives of each four-year college you're interested in

- go to college information sites such as:

    http://nces.ed.gov/collegenavigator/

    The *College Navigator* site makes it easy to find out information on four-year colleges including estimated student expenses, financial aid percentages and amounts, enrollment demographics, admission percentages and GPA/test scores, retention and graduation rates, available programs and majors, sports programs, accreditation and crime statistics. As with any information on four-year colleges, talk with the counselors at the colleges to see if there is more current information available.

www.utexas.edu/world/univ/alpha

This site lists U.S. four-year colleges in alphabetical order.

www.utexas.edu/world/univ/state

This site lists U.S. four-year colleges by state.

http://collegesearch.collegeboard.com/search/index.jsp

This site has a college matchmaker.

www.collegeboard.com

This site has a college search feature.

www.clas.ufl.edu/au/

This is an index of American universities granting bachelor or advanced degrees.

www.princetonreview.com/default.aspx?uidbadge=%07

Click Explore for colleges.

www.students.gov

This comprehensive site includes college searches.

www.collegedirectorynetwork.com

This site has information on thousands of colleges.

www.usnews.com/usnews/edu/college/rankings/rankindex_brief.php

This site has data on what it considers to be the best colleges.

• look at state websites that have a wealth of data on their public four-year colleges such as:

www.assist.org

For California four-year colleges, click Exploring Majors, then click Explore Majors, then click Majors, then select your area of study from a list or keyword and finally, view which public institutions offer that major.

http://uctransfer.universityofcalifornia.edu

Look at this website if you are planning to transfer from a California community college to a University of California campus. It can help you select a major and a campus to attend.

www.californiacolleges.edu

This is the official source for college and career planning in California.

www.csumentor.edu/AboutMentor/mentor.asp

This site is a California online resource designed to help students and their families learn about the California State University system, select a CSU campus to attend, plan to finance higher education and apply for admission.

http://regents.ohio.gov/colleges_universities.php (Ohio)

Click Colleges & Universities and then select what you want to view.

- look at an online library of thousands of college catalogs at *http://collegesource.org* — always go to the catalog on a college's website to double check the information listed on this site

- read the following college guides (even though they usually don't have much specialized information for transfer students):

Barron's Profiles of American Colleges

The College Board College Handbook

Fiske Guide to Colleges

Peterson's Four-Year Colleges

U.S. News & World Report Ultimate College Guide

In Step #5 in the next chapter you'll research each of the six four-year colleges on your list. If you like the answers you get, go on to Step #6 and ask more detailed questions. If you don't like the answers you get in Steps #5 or 6, keep adding four-year colleges to your list until you have at least six that can pass *your* tests. Remember, before the four-year colleges get to evaluate you, you get to evaluate them.

Chapter 12

Step #5: Research the Admission, Transfer and Graduation Requirements

You're probably thinking, "I understand why I would research the *admissions and transfer requirements* but why should I bother to look at the *graduation requirements* before I apply to a four-year college?" The answer is that seeing which courses (and how many of them) are required to graduate could influence your decision whether to even apply to that four-year college. Not only will you see the types and content of the courses, you'll be able to determine how long it will take (and cost) to graduate from that college. It's better for you to figure all of this out *before* you apply to a four-year college.

Stay organized

You'll soon see a list of questions to ask about each of your top picks for four-year colleges. You should keep all the questions and answers together in a written format via a spreadsheet or a word processing file (using the table function). You could also use the fill-in Admission/Transfer/Graduation chart at the end of this chapter (and then just photocopy it as many times as necessary). The chart isn't as useful as the spreadsheet or the table function in your word processing program because it can't automatically expand to have all of the information you may want to include. A better idea is to select the most pertinent questions for you and type them into your own spreadsheet or word processing file so you can add answers of any length (and any additional questions).

Whatever method you use, if you find an answer on the Internet, also copy the URL (the address where you found the information on the Internet) onto the chart, spreadsheet or word processing table so you can easily return to that Web page, if needed. Also, back up the information you find on an external drive and online (via an email to yourself with an attached file).

Since it can be difficult to remember all the details you're investigating, charting out the details makes it easier to do a side-by-side comparison of various colleges and programs if you keep a written record of all the four-year colleges you research. Some of the earlier ones that you ruled out could end up looking better by comparison as time goes on. If you have written down and kept the information on all of the four-year colleges you've researched, it's easy to go back to compare and even reconsider an earlier discarded choice.

A dozen questions to ask

The best ways to get the transfer information you need are by talking with your community college counselor, visiting the website of each four-year college you're researching and then confirming that information by a phone call, in-person visit or email to a counselor at the four-year college (and make a note of the date and the person's name, email address, phone number and title). Since information can change at any time, your final step should be to verify that information with a four-year college admission counselor or transfer coordinator.

Transfer coordinators / transfer counselors / transfer directors
A *transfer coordinator* (also sometimes called a *transfer coordinator* or *transfer director*) helps community college transfer students select the right courses, provides information on course and/or program transferability and assists students who want to appeal a denial of transfer credit.

Maryland lists both four-year and community college transfer coordinators at *www.mhec.state.md.us/preparing/stuguide.asp#What*. New Jersey on one web page (*www.njtransfer.org/html/contacts.asp?mu=menu_student&mn=contacts&vmode=stud ent*) lists the names and email addresses for the transfer contacts at all the state colleges and universities. Four-year colleges often have on their sites a list of their admission counselors organized by geographic area or community college. For example, the University of Southern California posts a list of counselors (*www.usc.edu/admission/undergraduate/prepare/counselor_profiles.html*).

Here are the key questions to ask for each four-year college:

1. Does the four-year college take transfer students?

This may seem like a silly question to ask but not all four-year colleges accept transfer students. If the answer is no, start looking elsewhere for another four-year college.

2. Can freshman, sophomores, juniors and seniors transfer in?

Many four-year colleges only accept junior transfers. Some accept sophomores and even freshmen. There can be a problem at certain four-year colleges if you have too many units (i.e., you're considered a senior). It usually depends on whether you've attended another four-year college in addition to going to community college(s). For example, if you first attended a four-year college, then switched to a community college and now want to attend a second four-year college, you may have too many units to be allowed to transfer. The key is to ask the four-year colleges about any unit limitation on admission and to let them know every two- and four-year college you've attended (and the order in which you've attended them). The same unit limitation may not apply if you've only attended community colleges. Ask a four-year college counselor to know how the rules apply to your situation.

3. When is there a better chance of admission—as a sophomore or as a junior?

Even if a four-year college accepts freshmen, sophomores and juniors, they may have a preference regarding the year you're entering the college.

4. During which semester or quarter may transfer students start taking courses?

Some four-year colleges allow transfer students to start taking courses during any semester or quarter of the school year while others only allow admission in the fall.

5. What are the admission requirements for a transfer student at the four-year college?

When you make your inquiries, make it clear that you're a transfer student. If you're applying to an out-of-state public four-year college, also let them know you're a non-resident of that state.

The admission requirements for transfer students may include *some or all* of the following:

- completing a minimum number of *transferable* college credits (units) in order to apply (find out if it's semester units or quarter units)

- completing a minimum number of transferable college credits (units) to be admitted (find out if it's semester units or quarter units)

- not exceeding a maximum number of community college and/or four-year college credits (units)—the maximum may vary at each four-year college and it may depend on whether you already took courses at another four-year college

- completing a minimum number of semesters at a community college before transferring if you've already attended another four-year college

- having the last college attended be a community college (possibly in that state)

- getting a minimum grade (e.g., find out if it's a C or C-) in each community college course to get transferable credit at the four-year college

- having a minimum overall GPA (grade point average) in all your community college courses to be admitted to the four-year college

- completing certain lower-division coursework in your major at community college

- having a minimum GPA in your lower-division coursework in your major

- completing certain General Education (GE) coursework at community college

- having a foreign language proficiency through courses at high school and/or community college

- submitting a portfolio of your work (e.g., as an artist)

- submitting letters of recommendation

- having a minimum GPA for high school courses

- scoring high enough on the SAT and/or ACT (find out if you have to take either of these tests)

- having a high school diploma or a GED or a proficiency certificate (e.g., CHSPE)

- having an A.A. (Associate of Arts) or other degree from community college

- meeting other requirements/possibilities (e.g., allowing you to get credit for a course by passing an AP [Advanced Placement], IB [International Baccalaureate] or CLEP [College-Level Examination Program®] exams.

With AP tests, ask both your community college and four-year college counselors exactly what your AP test scores will mean on the college level. For example, even if your scores get you course credit at community college, they may only give you unit credit but *not* course credit at a four-year college. In other words, you may still need to take a course where you've already taken and passed the AP test. How your AP scores count may depend on how high your test scores are. For credit from IB tests, find out from a counselor at a four-year college if you must have HL (High Level) testing results. For AP, IB and CLEP tests, ask a counselor what your test results mean for you as far as four-year college credits and courses.

6. What are the admission requirements to get admitted into your major?

The requirements for admission to the major may not be the same as admission to the four-year college. For example, a higher GPA (grade point average) in community college courses may be required for certain majors. So, although you might be able to get into a four-year college, you might not qualify for the major you want.

You also need to find out which lower-division coursework in your major you must take at community college to be admitted into your major. Different four-year colleges offering the same major may require very different (or no) lower-division coursework.

Also, it's possible that your community college does not offer all of the required lower-division coursework in your major. Unless you can find another way to take those courses (e.g., online or at another community college), you won't be able to meet those requirements at that community college. Your state may have a centralized list of all online courses in the state. For example, in California see the California Virtual Campus (*www.cvc.edu*) which is organized by courses, programs and schools.

Another possibility is the sequence and order of lower-division coursework in your major may mean that you'll have to spend considerable extra time at community college taking those courses before you can be admitted to the four-year college.

7. What General Education courses need to be taken at community college to be admitted to the four-year college?

Although probably every four-year college has English and math General Education requirements, beyond that there is no one set of required arts, humanities, foreign language and science courses. For example, some may require one science course while others may require two. You need to see what's required at each four-year college.

8. If you're admitted into the four-year college, what courses in (and for) your major will you be required to take at the four-year college?

Before you apply to a four-year college, check out the undergraduate degree requirements. Take a look at the courses you'd be taking in your major at the four-year college if you're admitted. Do they look interesting to you? Do you think you can handle those courses? As mentioned earlier, you might want to be a computer programming major until you realize all of the calculus and calculus-related courses you'd need to take. What you don't want is to start on a path of preparation for a major that won't work for you and then have to start all over taking other lower-division coursework for another major.

Also, sometimes there are "required electives" in addition to the required courses in the major. You don't want surprises after you're admitted that may require you to go to the four-year college for an extra semester or two. Now is the time to understand all the requirements if you're admitted.

9. If you're admitted into the four-year college, what General Education and other non-major courses will you be required to take at the four-year college?

Besides the General Education courses you may need to take while you're in community college, there may also be General Education and other required courses outside of your major that you'll have to take *at* the four-year college. You need to see what those courses are and how many of them you'll need to take. That could influence your decision to attend that college and how long it will take (and cost) to graduate from that college.

10. What is the maximum number of transferable units that can apply toward graduation?

Usually, there is not a big variance between schools. However, differences between competing four-year colleges may mean you can complete your college education quicker at one four-year college than another, depending on the credits you receive for your community college coursework.

11. How many units does it take to graduate from the four-year college?

Colleges usually require between 120 and 130 *semester* units. It can be higher. That's equal to 180 to 195 *quarter* units. College is expensive and your time is valuable. If the requirements for one particular four-year college mean that you will need to spend extra time to graduate as compared with another college, that may be too high a price to pay.

12. What is the earliest month/year you can graduate from the four-year college?

Once you evaluate the transfer credits you'll receive for your community college work and the remaining required courses and units to graduate from the four-year college, calculate the earliest date you'll be able to graduate taking a full load of courses at the four-year college.

The Admission/Graduation Chart starts on page 53. When you are done getting answers about a four-year college, add an overall numerical rating (from 1 to 10 with 10 being high) near the top of the chart together with any special comments and concerns so you can later recall your thoughts and feelings about the college.

If you don't like the answers to the dozen questions in this chapter, go back to Chapter 11 to come up with college(s) to replace the one(s) you've ruled out and then repeat the questions in this chapter.

Admission/Transfer/Graduation Chart

Names of four-year colleges:		
Name of your major		
Your overall numerical rating of the college from 1 to 10 (with 10 being high after completing the following 12 questions)		
Special comments/ concerns about the college (including research in Step #4, Chapter 11)		
Admission: timing		
1. Accepts transfer students?		
2a. Accepts freshmen, sophomores and juniors?		
2b. Has unit limit on accepting transfers (e.g., no seniors) and does the limit only apply if student has also already attended a four-year college?		
3. Better to apply as a sophomore or a junior?		

College names:		
Admission requirements		
4. What month/year can you start taking courses?		
5. What are the admission requirements for the college?		
a. Minimum # of transferable units to apply?		
b. Minimum # of transferable units to be admitted?		
c. Minimum grade in a course to get transferable credit?		
d. Minimum required overall GPA at community college?		
e. Foreign language requirement?		
f. Portfolio needed?		
g. Number of letters of recommendation needed?		
h. Need minimum GPA for high school courses? If yes, what GPA?		
i. Need SAT/ACT scores? If yes, minimum scores?		
j. Need high school diploma or GED or high school proficiency exam certificate?		

College names:		
k. Need A.A. or other Associate degree?		
l. Other requirements or options?		
6. What are the admission requirements for the major including GPA and required lower-division courses to be taken at community college?		
GE courses to take at community college		
7. What GE courses need to be taken at community college?		

College names:		
Required courses to take at the four-year college		
8. What courses in/for your major need to be taken at the four-year college?		
9. What GE and other non-major courses need to be taken at the four-year college?		

College names:		
Graduation		
10. What is the maximum number of community college transferable units and units from another four-year college that can apply toward graduation?		
11. How many semester/quarter units does it take to graduate?		
12. What is the earliest month/year you can graduate from the four-year college?		

Once you like the answers from six four-year colleges, give those colleges a final exam by asking the questions in Chapter 13.

Chapter 13
Step #6: Ask the Right Questions for You

Attending a four-year college is a major step in your life and a major investment, too. That's why it's worthwhile making the best choices you can. Take the time to select and ask the questions in this chapter that are most important to you and you'll have a much better idea whether a particular four-year college is right for you. And that is the point of this whole process—to find the four-year colleges that are the *best fit for you*.

You'll find the answers to some of these questions on the websites of the four-year colleges and others on the *College Navigator* website (*http://nces.ed.gov/collegenavigator/*). For many of the questions, you'll need to talk to counselors, professors, students, alumni and people working in the profession of your major.

Since four-year college requirements can change at any time, check with counselors each semester so you're aware of any new requirements. You may want to get advice from more than one counselor at your community college *and* at the four-year colleges you want to attend.

To keep track of the answers to these questions, it's a good idea to use a spreadsheet or a word processing file (using the table function). This will make it easier for you to do side-by-side comparisons of various four-year colleges and to reconsider an earlier discarded choice. You can use the spreadsheet or word processing file you created in Step #5 (Chapter 12) and add to it the questions in this chapter.

You can also use the fill-in chart in this chapter (and then just photocopy it as many times as necessary). The chart isn't as useful as the spreadsheet or the table function in your word processing program because it can't automatically expand to include all of the information you want. So, ideally type the questions shown in the chart into your own spreadsheet or word processing file so you can add all the answers you get (and any additional questions of your own).

Whatever method you use, if you find an answer on the Internet, also copy the URL (the address where you found the information on the Internet) onto the chart, spreadsheet or word processing table so you can easily return to that Web page, if needed, at a later date. Also, back up the information you find on an external drive and online (via an email to yourself with an attached file).

When you are done getting answers about a four-year college, add an overall numerical rating near the top of the chart and any special comments/concerns you have so you can later recall your feeling about the college.

Four-Year College Questions Chart

Names of four-year colleges:		
Name of your major		
Your overall numerical rating of the college from 1 to 10 (with 10 being high) after doing Steps 4-6 (Chapters 11-13)		
Special comments/concerns about the college		
Applications		
Is a separate application required for the department of the major?		
Deadlines		
What is the priority deadline for applying for admission to the four-year college?		
What is the priority deadline for applying for your major (it may not be the same deadline)?		
What is the priority deadline for applying to the college for financial aid?		
What is the priority deadline for applying for housing?		
Guaranteed Admission		
Is there a transfer admission guarantee program for Associate degree (e.g., A.A.) graduates or for students who sign a transfer admission guarantee contract (see Chapter 10)?		

College names:		
If yes, when does the transfer guarantee contract need to be signed?		
Cost		
How much are the yearly tuition and fees? (Don't use cost as a deciding factor yet. There may be extra financial aid available from more expensive four-year colleges so the cost may not end up being higher (or much higher) than others you are considering.)		
Is there lower or no tuition cost if income is below a specified level?		
If yes, for what level(s) of income?		
How much is the yearly cost of off-campus housing?		
How much is the yearly cost of on-campus housing?		
What is the total estimated cost for tuition, fees, books and housing until you graduate? Answer this question last after you've determined later in this chart how many years it'll take at the four-year college to graduate.		
Uniqueness / Reputation/ Educational Philosophy		
What is unique about your major at this college?		
What is unique about this college?		

College names:		
What is the reputation of your major at this college?		
What is the reputation of the college in general?		
What is the educational philosophy of your major at this college?		
What is the educational philosophy of the college?		
Has the educational philosophy of the major or college changed in the last 10 years? If so, how?		
Admission		
Are you admitted to your major or is another application to your major department required after you're admitted to the four-year college?		
Last year, what was the number and percentage of transfer students offered admission into your major at the four-year college?		
Last year, what was the number and percentage of transfer students offered admission into the four-year college?		

College names:		
Where does the four-year college place the most emphasis in evaluating transfer students for admission—by overall community college grades, by grades in lower-division coursework in your major, by high school grades, SAT and/or ACT scores, essays, portfolio or outside activities?		
How does the department of your major evaluate transfer students for admission?		
Who makes the transfer admission decision? The department of the major? The college's admission office? Both?		
What is the minimum grade for a community college course to count for transfer credit at the four-year college?		
Is it the same minimum grade for courses in your major, for GE courses and for elective credit?		
What is the four-year college's limit on the number of W's (withdrawals) from community college courses?		
What is the four-year college's limit on the number of courses that can be taken at community college on a pass/no-pass (credit) basis?		
Based on all the two- and four-year colleges you've attended, do you have too many units to be allowed to transfer to the four-year college?		
What is the limit on the total number of units of community college and four-year college transferable units that can apply to a bachelor's degree at the four-year college?		

College names:		
Does the four-year college prefer or require that you be a full-time student at community college?		
Will the four-year college evaluate your community college credits for transferability *before* you apply and when will you receive an official report and confirmation?		
Is credit given for AP, IB and CLEP tests?		
For AP tests, is there a minimum test score to get four-year college credit?		
Will an AP test score just get unit credit at the four-year college or will it also waive a specific course?		
For IB tests, must they be HL (High Level) tests to get four-year college credit?		
Will an IB test score just get unit credit at the four-year college or will it also waive a specific course?		
Last year, what were the average GPA and test scores of transfer students admitted to your major?		
Last year, what were the average GPA and test scores of transfer students admitted to the college?		
Academics		
How is the academic workload and pressure in your major?		
How is the academic workload and pressure at the college?		
Is the college on the semester system or the quarter system?		
When are the classes taught (day, evening and online) and at what locations (some four-year colleges have multiple campuses spread throughout a city)?		

College names:		
What is the faculty/student ratio in your major?		
What is the faculty/student ratio at the college?		
Are undergraduate courses in your major generally taught by a faculty member or a teaching/graduate assistant (TA)?		
Are other undergraduate courses generally taught by a faculty member or a teaching/graduate assistant (TA)?		
What is the average class size for courses in your major?		
What is the average class size for other courses?		
What percentage of students in your major go on to graduate school?		
What percentage of students in the college go on to graduate school?		
How many GE courses will you need to take at the four-year college? What are they?		

College names:		
How many lower-division major courses will you need to take at the four-year college? What are they?		
How many upper-division major courses will you need to take at the four-year college? What are they?		
How many other courses will you need to take at the four-year college? What are they?		

College names:		
How many years at the four-year college will it take for you to graduate?		
Your major		
Is your major scheduled for any cutbacks?		
Do you have to select a major before transferring?		
Can a major be changed once you're admitted? If so, how easy or difficult is it to change a major?		
What is the most popular major and why?		
What new majors are being planned?		
Can you design your own major?		
Demographics		
What is the total number of students at the four-year college?		
What is the number of undergraduate students in your major?		
What is the number of undergraduate students at the four-year college?		
What is the ratio of men to women in your major?		
What is the ratio of men to women at the college?		
How diverse are the students in your major?		
How diverse are the students at the college?		
How do you feel about the size and composition of the college?		
What percentage of the students live on campus?		
What percentage of the students commute to the college?		

College names:		
How close is the college to your home?		
What is the retention rate (the percentage of students who return for a second year)?		
What percentage of freshmen graduate in four years?		
What percentage of freshmen graduate in five years?		
What percentage of freshmen graduate in six years?		
How long on average does it take for transfer students to graduate once they're admitted?		
The Campus		
How safe are the campus and surrounding community? Call the Campus Police, local police and the Dean of Students' office at each college and ask about the prevalence of on-campus or campus-related drinking, drugs and violence. Also, take a look at the crime statistics shown for this college on the *College Navigator* website: *http://nces.ed.gov/collegenavigator/*		
Is there an alcohol/drug problem on campus and what is the college doing about it?		
Is this a wellness (substance-free) campus?		
What is the size and location of the nearest city to campus and the nearest large city to campus?		
What are the extracurricular activities, special interest groups and athletics at the college?		

College names:		
What are the most popular campus activities?		
Where is the center of the campus social life?		
Housing and meals		
What is the cost of off-campus housing?		
How easy or difficult is it to find affordable off-campus housing?		
How close is the available off-campus housing?		
How convenient are the markets and stores to the off-campus housing?		
What is the cost of on-campus housing?		
With on-campus housing, can you specify *and* actually be matched up with someone who is like you (e.g., studious, a quiet roommate)?		
How easy is it to switch roommates or to move to another room if there is a problem with a roommate?		

College names:		
What would the cost be if you had to move out of the dorm early because the roommate situation was intolerable?		
Is there a wellness dorm that's substance free?		
Is there any other information you can get on the housing options that would help you make your choice?		
How easy or difficult is it to get on-campus housing?		
Is there usually a waiting list to get on-campus housing?		
How many students are usually on the waiting list?		
Is there priority for transfer students for on-campus housing?		
Is there on-campus housing just for your major?		
Is there on-campus housing just for transfer students?		
What are the available meal plans and how much do they cost?		
Can you change a meal plan after you start a semester?		
Do the meal plans cover special food needs such as vegetarian or kosher?		
Health Insurance		
Is student health insurance available through the college?		
Can anyone get the insurance regardless of pre-existing conditions?		
What restrictions are there on the coverage?		
Can full-time *and* part-time students get the coverage?		
What is the cost and maximum amount of coverage?		

College names:		
Can a spouse, domestic partner and children be covered?		
Accreditation		
Is the college *regionally* accredited? Ask the counselors at your community college and four-year college.		
Specialized Services		
Are there specialized services (e.g., academic counseling, career counseling, pre-professional and pre-graduate school counseling tutoring, networking, socializing or child care) set up for all students and any especially for transfer students?		
Weather		
Ask about the weather—ask someone who comes from your part of the country or world how they've coped with the weather.		

If you're really looking ahead, you might want to look up the ratings of the professors in your major on college professor rating sites (such as *www.ratemyprofessors.com* or possibly student ratings or forums on each individual four-year college's website). This might give you a better feel for your major. Keep in mind that any rating service can give results that are biased or not how you would rate the same professor.

Finally, run your list of four-year colleges by your community college counselor.

Once you like the answers given by at least six four-year colleges to the questions in the last two chapters, you are ready to plan your coursework so you can save time and money during your college years.

Chapter 14

Step #7: Take the Right Courses

This is the most important paragraph in this guide. To transfer successfully, you need to understand three concepts. First, it isn't enough to ask whether a course is transferable. What is more important is whether a course is *articulated*. Courses you take at community college that are articulated courses do *more than* just transfer to a four-year college. Articulated courses at community college transfer *and* fulfill General Education and/or lower-division major requirements at a four-year college. Second, you need to know whether the four-year colleges you want to attend are more interested in your taking lower-division major courses or completing the General Education requirements at community college. Third, double-check the information you get (see pages 36 and 37). Talk to community college and four-year college counselors about the courses to take—don't rely just on online or print catalogs since information can change at any time.

If you don't plan your coursework with these three concepts in mind, you may not be admitted to a four-year college, you may be admitted to a college but not in your major and/or you may have to spend extra semesters or years at community college and/or the four-year college to fulfill requirements.

Elective courses that transfer do give you elective units towards graduation at a four-year college. These courses may be very useful to you in college and later in life.

Problems with taking too many total units

There are three ways taking too many units overall before you transfer could cause problems for you.

First, you may not get credit for all of the units you take. Before you sign up for too many electives at community college, keep in mind there is an overall limit on how many units will transfer from a community college to a four-year college (the number varies by college).

Second, and more importantly, in some cases depending on whether you've also already attended another four-year college, some four-year colleges won't let you transfer if you have too many total units. Ask a counselor at the four-year college what the maximum number of units is for your particular college background (i.e., all the two- and four-year colleges you've attended).

Third, you may use up your financial aid by taking courses that won't transfer or not count for General Education and/or lower-division major requirements.

The difference between transferable and articulated courses

Each course you take at community college will be treated in one of three ways at a four-year college:

- as a *transferable* course
- as an *articulated* course
- as neither a transferable course nor an articulated course — in other words, as a *nontransferable course*

Every articulated course is transferable but not every transferable course is articulated. Both types of courses get unit credit at a four-year college. But an articulated course is a transferable course on steroids — it gets credit toward a bachelor's degree at a four-year college (i.e., it is transferable) *and* it fulfills a General Education requirement, a requirement of a major or both.

In other words, every time you take an articulated course at community college, you are getting closer to *fulfilling the requirements* of earning a bachelor's degree. That reduces the time and cost of going to college. Although electives generally also earn you units towards graduation, make sure you are making good progress on your required courses.

Before you sign up for a course at community college, find out whether a course is *transferable*, *articulated* or *nontransferable*.

Transferable courses

Most community college courses are transferable to a four-year college and will get you units toward a bachelor's degree, at least as an elective course. But depending on the course and the requirements of a four-year college, a transferable community college course *may or may not* fulfill a General Education requirement *or* a requirement for your major.

A transferable course gets credit toward a bachelor's degree at a four-year college as:

1. a required General Education (GE) course *and/or*
2. a required course in your major *or*
3. an elective course (electives don't get GE or major credit)

Articulated courses

The term *articulated course* can have two meanings: (1) a course at one college that is equivalent to a course at another college and/or (2) a course by itself or in combination with other courses that satisfies a General Education and/or lower-division major requirement. You're generally more interested in the second meaning.

Not all community college courses are even transferable
Most community college courses are transferable to a four-year college. However, four-year colleges set their own requirements in determining whether a course is sufficiently challenging or consistent with their curriculum. Just because a course is listed in a community college catalog does not mean that it will get transfer credit at a four-year college.

Not all four-year college courses are transferable
If you've previously attended another four-year college, the four-year college to which you want to transfer may not accept all of your four-year college credits (units). You are more likely to have this problem if you went to a private four-year college, you are now going to a community college and you want to go to a public four-year college. Also see page 73 for issues on having too many units to even be able to transfer to some four-year colleges.

How do you know if a course is articulated?

The best sources of information on articulation are:

- an *articulation agreement* (an agreement of transferability and credit) on the website of the four-year college or a state-wide website
- an admissions counselor at the four-year college
- your community college counselor

You can't fully rely on the transfer/articulation information in a community college online or hardcopy catalog because that information can change at any time and may not be up to date.

Links for articulation and transfer websites

Links to the articulation and transfer websites for each state are at
www.aacrao.org/pro_development/transfer.cfm

Another possible tool is u.select, an online tool designed to help you view
program requirements and course equivalencies and see how courses you've
taken or plan to take transfer to certain four-year colleges
(*http://clients.redlanternu.com/home/display/USL/u.select*).

Types of articulation agreements

There are individual articulation agreements between a community college and a
given four-year college and also more universal agreements, too. In some cases,
there will be neither an individual articulation agreement nor a universal
articulation agreement regarding your community college and your chosen four-
year college.

Six types of agreements and programs

1. Individual agreement between a community college and a four-year (public or private) college

> If you have a specific four-year college in mind, first see whether there is a
> direct *articulation agreement* with your community college. That's the
> easiest way to determine how your community college coursework will be
> treated by the four-year college. Go to the website of the four-year college
> to search for "transfer," "transfers" or "articulation" to find an agreement
> with your community college. Also get advice from your college
> counselors.

2. Statewide public college GE (General Education) articulation agreement

> Some states have agreements where taking the specified list of GE courses

at a public community college will automatically satisfy all of the GE requirements at a four-year *public* college in the same state. One example of this is the *IGETC* (Intersegmental General Education Transfer Curriculum) in California (*www.assist.org/web-assist/help/help-igetc.html* and *www.igetc.org*). The California State University LDTP program (see page 36 takes it a step further by providing a road map for both GE *and* major courses. Arizona has the AGEC, the Arizona General Education Curriculum (*www.aztransfer.com/TransferBasics*).

With the Illinois Articulation Initiative, all colleges and universities participating in the IAI agree to accept a "package" of IAI general education courses in lieu of their own comparable lower-division general education requirements (*www.itransfer.org/container.aspx?file=iai*). The IAI General Education transfers as a *package*. Course-to-course transfer is not guaranteed. IAI also includes recommendations for major courses.

These types of agreements do *not* guarantee your admission to a particular major. To get into the major you want, you might still need to take lower-division coursework in your major and meet other requirements.

By the way, if you attend more than one community college, you may want to have the other community college(s) send an official transcript to the one community college that will be certifying you (e.g., for completion of the IGETC requirement) to a four-year college. That way the certifying community college will have all of your official transcripts necessary for the certification.

3. Major preparation agreements

A *major preparation agreement* between a community college and a four-year college spells out the lower-division courses you need to take at a community college to be accepted in the major at the four-year college. Courses may double count to fulfill General Education requirements, too.

4. Associate transfer degree

Some states offer transfer agreements where certain four-year public colleges will accept community college students from certain community colleges in that state who get an Associate degree (e.g., Associate of Arts) and maintain a specified minimum GPA (grade point average). Some transfer degrees include all the GE-required coursework at the four-year college while others also cover all required lower-division courses in a major.

5. Transfer admission guarantee agreements

These are different from #4 above. In some states, *transfer admission guarantee agreements* guarantee your admission to a public four-year college in your state if you sign a transfer admission guarantee (TAG) or transfer advantage program (TAP) contract, complete the specified General Education and lower-division coursework in your major at a community college in that state and maintain a specified minimum GPA (regardless of whether you get an Associate degree).

With an A.A. or other Associate transfer degrees or a TAG/TAP program, find out whether you're guaranteed admission to the four-year college as well as in a particular major through this program. To get the major you want, you might still need to take lower-division coursework in your major and meet other requirements.

6. Informal agreements

Even where there isn't a formal agreement between a community college and a four-year college, both schools may have information on their websites or through their counselors indicating the recommended courses to take to transfer from one school to another.

Contact transfer coordinators / transfer counselors / transfer directors

You can also contact the transfer coordinators (also known as transfer counselors and transfer directors) at the four-year colleges you're interested in and have them review a list of the courses you've taken and/or will be taking before entering the four-year college. Make your list more complete by including not only the course descriptions and course numbers from your community college's catalog but also trying to match up your courses as much as possible with the four-year college's courses. That will reduce the work for the transfer coordinator and make it easier to give you a response. Ideally communicate via email so you'll have a written record.

Your best strategy for taking courses

Your best strategy for deciding which community college coursework to take will vary depending on your major and the four-year colleges you select. The ideal strategy is to take all required lower-division coursework in your major and all required General Education (GE) courses. But that may not be possible or even necessary. Find out whether the four-year colleges you're interested in want you to take community college GE courses or lower-division courses in your major. Finally, see if you can take any courses that double count as GE *and* lower-division major coursework.

Going part-time vs. full-time

Take at least some courses each semester so you don't lose your momentum. Although most community college students go part-time, you may want to try full-time enrollment for several reasons. This will not only reduce your time in school but for some four-year colleges it is one of the requirements for admission—to show that you can handle a full academic load. Also, research shows that full-time students are more likely to transfer.

But most importantly, know yourself. You may be better off taking fewer units or working fewer hours in your job, especially during your first semester, to reduce stress and avoid exhaustion. If possible, give yourself time to learn good study habits (including how to take notes in class and take exams) and to get used to community college life.

Tips for selecting courses

- Find out if a course is transferable or articulated before you take it.

- Check with the four-year college(s) to get the best answer on transfer/articulation credit—allow enough time for a response before your class sign-up date.

- When choosing between two courses, see if one will satisfy requirements at multiple four-year colleges you're considering.

- See whether a course can meet multiple requirements (such as both a lower-division course in your major and as a GE course—for example, if you're a psychology major, Psychology 1 *may* do double duty).

- Although electives can help you discover your major/field of interest, four-year colleges have limits on how many overall units can be transferred. There is a risk that elective courses may not count at all if the overall unit limit is exceeded.

- Choose your classes wisely and keep track of your overall college unit total—remember that some four-year colleges won't let you transfer if you have already attended another four-year college and a community college and have taken "too many" total units.

- Find out whether there's a limit on how many units will transfer in particular subject areas such as performance courses (e.g., music).

- Ask counselors at the community college and the four-year colleges whether your military education and experience will get you college credit.

- Determine whether your course(s) are considered as technical/vocational/occupational courses that may not receive any transfer credit.

- Ask the four-year colleges whether your units are "too old" — if you took courses some time ago especially in areas that change rapidly, you might find that your units won't be counted by some four-year colleges. For colleges that may give you credit, you may need to provide a catalog course description, a syllabus, sample papers you wrote and other documentation to prove that credit should still be given.

- Check the current articulation agreement on the four-year college website before signing up for a course — a course may be treated as fulfilling a requirement one year but not the next year.

- See how many foreign language courses are required with one major (and one four-year college) as compared with another.

- The required GE courses at the four-year college may depend on the major you've selected.

General Education requirements are sometimes called *core requirements*, *core classes* or *general university requirements*. The GE requirements, at a minimum, usually include English composition, mathematics, natural (biological and physical) sciences, behavioral and social sciences, arts and the humanities.

There are several reasons why colleges want you to take GE courses. First, GE courses may spark your interest in a major that might not otherwise have occurred to you. Second, you'll want to develop skills that are transferable in the work world. The major you're studying today could become obsolete or have reduced demand for employment over your work life. The skills you'll learn in GE courses such as critical thinking, problem solving and effective communication in a diverse, global economy will help you no matter where you're working.

Just as the lower-division and upper-division courses in a major vary from college to college, so do the General Education courses. And just as lower-division major courses may satisfy requirements at multiple four-year colleges, so may the GE courses you take.

Also, ask the four-year college how your GE courses will be treated if you complete some, but not all, of the GE requirements.

- Some states have a universal course numbering system to make it easier to know that a particular course at a community college is the same course at public four-year colleges in the same state. One such state is Florida (see *http://scns.fldoe.org/scns/public/pb_index.jsp*). Other states have a transfer information system; one such state is California (see *www.assist.org)*.

- Don't procrastinate when it comes to registering for courses—study the community college catalog and class schedules and do some homework on researching the professors (see *www.ratemyprofessors.com*) before the signup time for classes.

- Some courses are only offered once a year so don't miss signing up for them.

- If there are multi-semester, sequential courses you need to take, make it a priority to sign up as early as possible for the first course in the sequence (you may need to take all of the courses in the sequence to get credit for fulfilling a requirement).

- Register early, too, for courses with very limited enrollment spaces or for courses that are very popular.

- Be persistent in finding courses that are difficult to locate in a catalog; they just might be listed in a different department (e.g., a political philosophy course may be listed under Political Science, Philosophy or in both places).

- If you need a course not offered by your community college, see if you can find it online (in California, see the California Virtual Campus at *www.cvc.edu* which is organized by courses, programs and schools). Before you sign up for a course, check with your college counselors to make sure the course will work for you.

- If you're really set on going to a particular four-year college, maybe you should take summer school or extension courses at the college to demonstrate your level of interest in the college and your capability of handling the coursework and stress these efforts in your application. Find out the transfer credit policy on summer school and extension courses.

- Take courses at regionally accredited colleges.

Now that you know your major, the four-year colleges you'd like to attend and the courses you'll need to take to get there, it's time to dig deeper into money issues so you'll be able to afford the rest of your college career.

Chapter 15
Step #8: Find the Money to Attend a Four-Year College

Now is the time to take another look at the money issues—costs, scholarships, grants, loans and other financial aid. You may also want to review the discussion in Chapter 9 about sticker prices vs. net prices and how long it takes on average to graduate from a four-year college.

Ways to reduce college costs

College is expensive but completing your education at a four-year college may be more affordable than you think. By going to a community college, you are already saving a lot on college tuition. And, if you transfer as a junior, you'll save even more money.

Here are some other ways to reduce the four-year-college cost:

- Look for less costly colleges and universities. Paying a higher tuition is no guarantee of a higher quality education. Four-year *public colleges* are generally less expensive than four-year *private colleges. In-state* public colleges are generally less expensive than *out-of-state* public colleges. (If you go out of state to a public four-year college, that may mean paying higher, non-resident tuition.)

- Some four-year colleges lower the tuition or reduce it to zero depending on family income levels.

- Some four-year colleges will give you more articulated and/or transfer credits for your community college coursework than other four-year colleges. That affects how long you'll be attending a four-year college and how much your education (and housing) will cost there.

- Many four-year colleges allow their students to get credit for summer classes taken at a community college. You may need advance permission to take a class. If a three-unit class at a four-year private college costs $3,000 vs. $60 in a summer class at a community college, it can really pay to pick up some units at a community college during the summer.

- If you took advance placement classes in high school, those classes *may* qualify for two- and four-year college credits. Depending on how high your test scores are, you may only receive college credit at the community college level or at both the community college and four-year college level. The four-year college level credit may only be for units and not waive a required course. This is an area where you may be in for an unpleasant surprise so be sure to check with both community college and four-year college counselors to see exactly what credit you'll receive.

- If you have taken IB (International Baccalaureate, *www.ibo.org*) tests, see whether HL (High Level) tests are required to get college credit and ask both a community college and four-year college counselor exactly what credit you'll receive.

- Make sure you and your parents take advantage of all available tax benefits connected with funding and paying for a college education.

- Use military service education benefits to pay for college.

- See if your military education and experience has already earned you college credit (*www.military.com/sitemap* –click College Credit for Service).

- Take advantage of nonmilitary service programs such as AmeriCorps (*www.americorps.org*) to obtain college assistance.

Also use the calculators and information at *www.fafsa4caster.ed.gov/*, *www.finaid.org* and *www.collegeboard.com* to help you budget and find ways to pay for college.

Scholarships and grants

Scholarships are given for all levels of profiles and talents (including special academic, artistic or athletic abilities) and *don't* need to be repaid. Scholarships can also be need-, merit- and affiliation-based. According to experts, many scholarships are never applied for so don't just look at online databases; be creative in searching for scholarships. Grants are financial aid, based on need, which you also *don't* have to repay. (The other main type of financial aid, loans, does need to be repaid.)

- Scholarship sites include:

    www.collegeanswer.com

    www.collegeboard.com

    www.fastweb.com

    www.finaid.org

    www.scholarships.com

    http://studentaid.ed.gov (click the Tools and Resources tab,
        look for Scholarship Search and click the "Go" button)

- Many four-year colleges have scholarships just for transfer students (e.g., Phi Theta Kappa—*www.ptk.org*). Usually, these are merit-based scholarships that are awarded on GPA and completion of a minimum number of units at a community college. These scholarships often require that you take a certain number of units at the four-year college and maintain a specified GPA for the scholarship to continue.

- Besides allowing you to possibly qualify for grants and loans, many scholarships at four-year colleges that are not need-based require that you file a FAFSA — the Free Application for Federal Student Aid (see below). Check the financial aid page of every school that you're applying to for details.

- If you apply to four-year colleges where you're more qualified than the average applicant, the schools are more likely to compete for you by offering a merit scholarship.

- Don't overlook state financial aid programs such as CAL Grants (*www.csac.ca.gov/default.asp*) in California.

- Some scholarships are on a first-come, first-served basis so apply as early as possible.

Qualifying for financial aid

Four items should be emphasized here. First, even if you were not eligible for financial aid at your community college, that doesn't mean you won't qualify for aid at a four-year college.

Second, financial aid can be affected by who owns the college savings. In general, it is usually better for parents to save in their names, not in a student's name. For financial aid purposes, student assets are generally assessed at a 20% rate each year as compared with a 5.64% rate for assets of parents, which means that for the same amount of savings, a student will pay more of his or her own funds toward tuition than the student's parents would.

Third, apply before the *priority deadlines*. Miss out on a priority deadline and you may transform free money that got away into a loan that you must repay. If a priority deadline has gone by, you should still apply even though you won't get priority consideration.

Fourth, filing a FAFSA is a must.

FAFSA

Be sure to apply to FAFSA (the Free Application for Federal Student Aid) no matter what your financial circumstances are. It's a free application and a free FAFSA report will be sent to all the four-year colleges you list on the FAFSA form. (There's no problem if you don't apply to a four-year college that's listed on your FAFSA.)

Read the directions carefully. Certain assets are exempt and should not be reported.

You may also want to use *FAFSA4caster* (*www.fafsa4caster.ed.gov/*), a great tool from Federal Student Aid (*www.FederalStudentAid.ed.gov*), an office of the U.S. Department of Education. It provides you and your family with an early estimate of eligibility for federal student aid, the expected family contribution and eligibility for a Pell grant (a needs-based federal grant to low-income college students). The forecasting tool is based on the *FAFSA*, the qualifying form for federal financial aid. You can also do estimated financial aid calculations at *www.finaid.org/calculators/finaidestimate.phtml*.

In general, you can get the FAFSA forms in November of each year at *www.fafsa.ed.gov*. However, the earliest you can submit your information is on January 1 for the year you're trying for aid (e.g., to apply for aid for the 2011-2012 school year, you'd apply on or after January 1, 2011). It's a good idea to start assembling the needed information before January.

After you file the FAFSA, you'll receive (and so will the colleges you list on your FAFSA) a Student Aid Report from the federal government stating the expected family contribution for your college expenses. If there has been a significant change of circumstances after you filed the FAFSA (or a difference between estimated and actual filed income tax information), you can amend your FAFSA.

CSS PROFILE

You may also need to submit financial aid forms to four-year colleges and complete the College Scholarship Service (CSS) Financial Aid Profile® (*https://profileonline.collegeboard.com/prf/index.jsp*). The exemptions on the CSS PROFILE form are different from those on the FAFSA form. Read the directions carefully. Four-year colleges may use their own method to determine financial aid eligibility.

Don't miss the financial aid deadlines

Deadlines are so important that you will read about them here, too. Always ask what the priority deadline is. If you meet a priority deadline, you get priority consideration. In these economic times, you want all the priority consideration you can get.

There are three possible deadlines:

- federal deadlines
- state deadlines
- four-year college deadlines

Make sure you know what the deadlines are. All of the deadlines may fall on different dates and may not be the same as four-year college application deadlines—financial aid applications may be due before the college applications. Some aid is available on a first-come, first-served basis so don't procrastinate.

To stay qualified for financial aid for the next school year, you may need to take a specified number of units and maintain a specified minimum GPA.

Responding to financial aid offers

Negotiate grants, costs and financial aid with the colleges. It doesn't hurt to ask whether you can qualify for more aid. This is especially true if your circumstances have changed since the FAFSA was filed. Private colleges generally have more flexibility to negotiate funding but it doesn't hurt to negotiate with public four-year colleges, too.

Changes in financial circumstances during the school year

If there is a change in your and/or your family's financial circumstances (e.g., a job loss, a pay cut, a death or extraordinary bills such as for medical care) during the school year, you may be able to get additional financial aid. Contact the college financial aid office to find out the procedure. It probably will involve writing a letter to the financial aid office asking for a review of your financial aid package and attaching any relevant documentation. Keep a record of what you send and you should probably send it via certified mail, return receipt requested.

Loans

Even if you don't qualify for financial aid, you may be able to get educational loans. At the time this book is being written, major changes to students loans are being proposed. Currently, there are Stafford Loans, PLUS loans, Sallie Mae Signature Student Loans, home equity loans and loans against a 401(k) plan. Loans vary in size, the interest rate, the tax deductibility of interest, the repayment period and how the family (and student) income and assets affect the amount available. Try to get federal loans before private loans.

There is a proposal for the federal government to make loans directly to students, bypassing private lenders. The financial aid office of a four-year college should be able to give you up-to-date information on lenders. Make sure you shop around to get the best deal and be sure to read and understand the paperwork before you sign anything. Try to minimize the size of your loans. If the amount of your student loans when you graduate is too large, it can put tremendous pressure on you and affect your choice of jobs and career due to the necessity of repaying the loans.

If it looks like the money and academic issues will work for you, you're ready to visit campuses to see whether the four-year colleges look good not only on paper but also in person. That's the next step.

Chapter 16
Step #9: Visit the Campuses

It can be costly to visit college campuses. But since choosing a college is a very important decision, it's a good idea to visit a campus before making a decision about attending a four-year college. (Virtual college tours are another, less expensive option—see below). You may decide to visit a campus *before* you apply or *after* you're accepted. Cost will obviously be a big factor affecting your decision.

You can arrange a campus visit through the admissions or recruitment office of a four-year college. To get the most from your visit, make a list of your questions ahead of time and make an appointment to speak with an academic advisor/counselor at the four-year college. To get more out of your visit, bring along a copy of your transcripts (high school and all college transcripts) and catalog course descriptions for the college courses you've taken and are planning to take.

Your on-campus visit itinerary

Go while school is in session so you get a real feel for the campus. Chances are you'll spend no more than a day (and maybe a night) on campus. Make the most of your time by prearranging what you want to see.

Arrange in advance to sit in on a class in your major and to talk with at least one professor in your major. Also meet with an advisor in your major. If you're a science major, see the labs. Visit the student union, library, and places where students hang out.

If you're planning on living off-campus, see the neighborhoods where students live and how accessible transportation is between off-campus housing and the campus. Call the local police station to find out about the crime statistics and relatively safety of the neighborhoods. Ask "Where would you let your daughter live?"

If you plan to live on campus, visit a dorm (or maybe stay there overnight) and try to eat a meal or two in the dorm dining hall. During your visit, ask other students what they like and dislike about the college, housing and food.

Questions to ask during your in-person campus visit

Take a look at the questions in Chapters 12 and 13. If any of those questions are still unanswered, now is the time to ask them again. Besides those questions and your own list of questions, make sure you ask:

- Where is the center of campus activities?

- How will I meet other transfer students?

- Are there any activities and services to help transfer students get settled socially and academically during the first transfer year?

- What are the housing options on-campus and off-campus?

- Where are the markets, movies and other services?

- What public transportation is available and how close is it to campus?

- Do most students have a car? Is it really necessary?

- Where is the student parking and what is the cost?

- How can I find an on-campus job?

Make some notes

As you go through your campus visit, write down your thoughts. This will help you keep a sense of perspective after you've visited several campuses and they begin to blur together. At the end of your visit, give the four-year college an overall rating from 1 to 10, with 10 being high.

Write down:

- any concerns you have about the college and/or the campus

- what impressed you the most

- what impressed you the least

- your thoughts on the students you met, the campus, the size of the campus, the housing options, the weather and anything else that comes to mind

Virtual college tours

With money always being tight, use a virtual college tour as a first step to narrow your search for the right four-year colleges. Look at sites such as:

- E-Campus Tours (*www.ecampustours.com*)

- Campus Tour (*www.campustours.com*)

- Youniversitytv (*www.youniversitytv.com*)

- Collegiate Choice Walking Tours DVD Videos (*www.collegiatechoice.com*)

Other ways to save money on campus visits

- Combine campus visits with vacation trips.
- Visit campuses that are relatively close to one another on the same trip.
- Look for student travel discounts on *www.studentuniverse.com* and *www.campusvisit.com*.

- Consider using a campus tour service (*www.cetours.com*).
- Some four-year colleges waive application fees if you make a campus visit and some will pay for part of your travel expenses. Ask the admissions office.

Now that you've selected your major and the four-year colleges where you want to transfer, it's time to do the applications. That's what the next chapter is all about.

Chapter 17
Step #10: Complete Your Transfer Applications

Applying to four-year colleges can be a time-consuming, expensive and exhausting process. Actually, it's designed that way in part to see who has the intelligence, tenacity and organization skills to navigate the process successfully. If you use all the tools in this guide, you'll get it done in an organized way that will save you time, money and aggravation.

Applying to a four-year college as a transfer student is not the same as applying as a high school student. In general, it is your community college academic record (especially in lower-division coursework in your major) that may be the most important factor to a four-year college in evaluating your application. That's why you want to buckle down and do your best in your community college studies. Although your application essays will be important, too, chances are that the extracurricular activities that are so important on a high school application will generally not be as important for your transfer application.

Having said that, you must be aware that all of your grades and every part of your application can make a difference as to whether you're admitted to a four-year college. If a college has two students with the same GPA and academic background and one spot is still available, then the application essays or another item can be the factor used to make a choice between the two students. Even the application process itself can be a test to see whether you can submit a complete application, transcripts, grammatically correct essays and all other necessary supplemental materials in a timely manner.

Four types of applications

1. The college's own application form

Most four-year colleges have their own application form.

2. A system-wide application

Some college systems (such as the California UC system) use one application for all of the campuses (e.g., UCLA, Berkeley, Davis, etc.). On the application, you are allowed to select your choices for the campuses you want to attend. If those choices don't work out, you may be assigned to another campus that has space.

3. The Common (Transfer) Application

Many four-year colleges use the Common Application (*www.commonapp.org*) instead of their own application form. Some colleges use it as their only application while others use it as the main form and add their own supplemental application. Note that transfer students and high school students have separate Common Application forms.

4. Applications to the department of a major

Don't forget that there may be a separate, additional application for the department of your major. This separate application may have its own deadline that's earlier, the same as or later than the main college application deadline date.

Apply ahead of deadline dates

There will be many separate parts to your application besides the application itself. Apply way in advance in case portions of your application package (e.g., transcripts, letters of recommendation, your portfolio, etc.) are lost or not received. This advanced planning will give you time to resubmit items and still meet deadlines. Also, if you're an international student, allow extra time because you will probably have to provide additional documentation and pass the TOEFL (Test of English as a Foreign Language — at *www.ets.org*, click TOEFL).

Another reason to apply earlier is that applications, scholarships, other financial aid and housing are often considered on a first-come, first-served basis.

When to apply

There are three application times to consider.

1. **Admission as a freshman, sophomore or a junior**

   Waiting to be admitted until your junior year may make you better prepared to handle the courses at the four-year college and also save you a lot on tuition. Also, if you apply as a junior, it is more likely that just your community college grades will be considered most strongly. If you apply to transfer as a freshman or sophomore, then it is more likely that your high school grades and SAT and/or ACT scores will be important, too.

2. **The four-year college application deadline — fixed or rolling**

   While most four-year colleges have just one deadline date for filing the main application, some four-year colleges have a *rolling admission* policy where you can apply at any time as a transfer student. While this policy is helpful if you want to apply later in the school year, rolling admission can be an invitation to procrastination and really cost you. If you wait too long to apply under a rolling admission policy, all the spots may fill and so it may be too late to submit an application that will result in admittance. Again, colleges may also apply this first-come, first-served process to housing and financial aid applications.

3. **The department major application deadline**

   Find out if you need to file a separate application with the department of your major in addition to the application to the four-year college. This department application may have a different deadline than the main college application.

Be sure to read the fine print to know whether a deadline is a "must be postmarked" or a "must be received by" deadline.

Organizing your essays

You may need to write several essays just for one four-year college. Multiply that by the different essays required by different colleges and major departments and you have a recipe for confusion.

That's why you'll want to set up a system for organizing your essays. It's a good idea to create a folder on your computer called *College Essays*. Within that folder, create subfolders for each college (e.g., one for USC and a separate one for University of Wisconsin).

Then, when you write a draft of an essay, save it with a name that will not only identify it by college and date but also by the version of the essay.

Here's an example of how folder, subfolder and essay file names could look:

Folder: College Essays

Subfolder: USC

Files:

USC Film Dept Application 9-21-2010 version 1

USC Film Dept Application 9-24-2010 FINAL

USC General Application 9-20-2010 version 1

USC General Application 9-30-2010 version 2

USC General Application 10-4-2010 FINAL

Make backups

As you go along, make sure you back up your draft and final essays on an external drive and print them out, too. It's also a good idea to have an off-site backup by saving it online or sending yourself an email (with the essay, draft or final, as the case may be) as an attached file.

Tips for writing the essays

Your essays are an important part of your application. You'll most likely have a chance to talk about yourself and tell your unique story, strengths, special talents and background. You may also get to tell why you are especially motivated to be in the major and attend this particular four-year college and why it's a very good fit for both you *and* the college. Finally, you may be able to deal with any issues in your academic history or special circumstances that need explaining (e.g., unexplained gaps in your studies or why you had lower grades during your earlier time in college).

Most importantly, *be yourself and make sure you're answering what an essay question is asking*.

- See if there's a college application essay writing workshop at your community college.
- Before you begin writing, brainstorm and outline your points.
- If you have writer's block, just talk your first draft to your computer if it has a recording feature—then you can play it back and type up what you said.
- Have a strong opening sentence and topic paragraph that grabs the reader and sparks an interest to read more.
- In the body of your essay, give facts and/or examples to support your topic or to prove your point.
- In your conclusion, tie the opening and body together and state your conclusion.

- Proof each draft, make edits and back up each draft with a new file name (e.g., USC General Application 9-30-2010 version 2).

- Keep making edits until you are happy with the result.

- If your computer has a speech function that can read your essay out loud to you, play back your essay so you're listening and reading a hard copy at the same time with a pencil in hand.

- Make additional edits and have at least two people with judgment you trust read and give you feedback.

- Then show your essay to a community college counselor for feedback.

- Make your final edits, have it read out loud to you (by your computer or someone else), save it with "FINAL" as part of the file name and back it up on an external drive and online (e.g., via an email attachment).

If appropriate, when answering a question tell why:

- studying your major will help you reach your career and life goals

- the four-year college would be a good fit for you and why you would be an asset to the four-year college

- your outside activities (jobs, volunteer work, internships, etc.) are relevant

- your grades have improved over time (colleges like to see that!)

- there are any educational time gaps between completing high school and the time of your application (make this a positive item by explaining how you are better prepared to go on to a four-year college)

Completing online applications

Since most applications are online applications, you'll want to be fully prepared before you log on to complete the application. That means you'll proof and spellcheck your essays (and have others read them) and organize them on your computer so you don't accidentally cut and paste from a draft essay instead of a final essay or an essay written for a different major or a different four-year college.

Fill in every item on an application—if the question doesn't apply to you, then fill in N/A (for not applicable).

Make sure you're using a secure computer since you will be typing in confidential information such as your date of birth and Social Security number. Make sure the computer has recently had an antivirus and an antispyware scan and that the browser (e.g., Internet Explorer, Firefox, Safari, etc.) has the latest security updates.

Keep track of your passwords for each college's application by printing or handwriting them and keeping them in a safe place.

Since applying to colleges can be an exhausting process, make sure you're well rested when you go through the online application process. Another tip is to make sure you have a high-speed Internet connection so you don't get timed out in the middle of an application.

Note on the application any name change you've had so transcripts and test scores can be matched up with your application.

If you have an option to print out your essays and application before you click to send it to the four-year college, do so. Then carefully read through the printout to catch any typos and to make sure you have the right essay(s) before clicking the send button. Once you apply, print out the confirmation that your application has been received and keep the confirmation in an accessible folder.

Be sure to pay the application fee.

Tracking progress of your applications

Track the progress of your application(s) over the Internet and/or via phone calls to the admissions office and/or the department of your major.

Even tracking the progress of your college application, department-of-your-major application and financial aid application can get confusing.

First, there may be separate online locations to check each application. Make sure you check all of them. Second, four-year colleges may have procedures where you fax in needed documents using special cover and closing page sheets that are coded to reflect the document you're faxing and the beginning and ending pages. You may, in turn, receive an automated email from the college acknowledging receipt of the faxed document. However, a college's tracking system may still show that the college did *not* receive a document even though you faxed it in and you received a confirmation email. You *must* keep going back to the four-year college's tracking locations to double check that all needed documents have been received before the deadline date. Each time a college's online tracking system shows that a particular application has been received in its entirety, it is a good idea to print out the screen shot that says this and keep this printout with your other important hard copy application documents.

Email communication to/from the four-year colleges

Since most four-year colleges communicate with students via email after an application is filed, be sure to check your email daily (including your spam folder) and respond by deadline dates.

Transcripts

As part of any application, you'll need to have transcripts sent from *every* community and four-year college you've attended showing all the college courses you've taken and your grades.

Find out whether the transcripts should be sent directly by your college(s) to each four-year college or whether you're supposed to turn them in attached to a transcript form as part of the application. Chances are you'll need to have official transcripts sent directly from the college(s) to the four-year colleges.

Find out whether official high school and military transcripts need to be sent, too.

Letters of recommendation

Some colleges do not require letters of recommendation. Others do. In some cases, the letters are required by the department of your major but not by the college itself.

In general, it is better if you can get a letter of recommendation from a community college professor in your major. That's another reason to decide as early as possible what your major will be so you'll be able to form a relationship with a professor who can later provide a letter of recommendation. You may also want to get letters of recommendation from other professors as well as a community college counselor.

Even if a four-year college or department does not require a letter of recommendation, it might be a good idea to have a strong letter submitted unless the college specifically says it does not want letters.

References who write you a letter of recommendation are doing you a favor. Make it as easy as possible for them by emailing a bio or resume about yourself and letting them know the college(s) and major you're interested in. Let your reference know your deadline for sending the letter (your deadline should be at least a week or two before the real college deadline) and find out whether it can be met.

Touch base with your reference about one week before your deadline to ask whether there's any additional information needed from you. The real purpose of this contact is to make sure the letter has been sent or will be sent on time.

Once the letter has been sent, send a thank you to the reference. Once you're admitted to the four-year college, let your reference know and send another thank you.

Portfolio

For a major in the arts and some other majors, you may also be required to submit a portfolio. The earlier you select your major and prospective four-year colleges, the sooner you can begin to produce the portfolio pieces you may need for your transfer application. If possible, keep backups of all portfolio pieces in a secure place.

The evaluation process by a four-year college

There is no one evaluation standard that applies to every four-year college. Look at a four-year college's website and talk to the admissions office to see how various factors are weighed when making a decision. If it comes down to a choice between you and another applicant, even if a four-year college usually only looks at college-level grades, the deciding factor may be your:

- interest in the four-year college and major as shown through your essays and interviews (that's another way a campus visit might help)
- involvement in the field of your major either through work, internships or volunteering
- personal/life experiences, employment and community involvement

What if you don't get in?

The process of applying to college(s) can be very stressful. Unfortunately, part of that process is not being accepted everywhere you'd like to be admitted. You should have a Plan B in case you don't get into the four-year college of your choice or don't get your preferred major.

Part of your Plan B should be applying initially to enough four-year colleges so that you're definitely qualified to get into at least one of your choices. However, if you're really set on going to just one particular four-year college and you weren't admitted, maybe you should take a different approach for getting admitted on a second try. Take extension or summer school courses at the college to demonstrate your level of interest in the college and your capability of handling the coursework and stress these efforts in your next application.

All you can do with applications is give them your best effort. You may not get into your "perfect" college. A rejection by a college is *not* a measure of your self-worth and for every door that closes in life, another one opens. Going to a particular college does not guarantee success in life, nor does it prevent it. Above all, you need to be a *great person* in life more than you need to graduate from a *great college*. And with nearly 3,000 four-year colleges in the U.S., there are many Plan B's for you.

Transfer Application Checklist

Note key deadline dates in bold (and highlight them, too) not only on this form but also on your paper-based and/or electronic calendars. Write "Yes" for every completed item and the completion date.

Names of four-year colleges		
Name of major		
Main application		
What does the four-year college use — its own application, a system-wide application and/or the Common Application (with or without a supplemental application)?		
Downloaded or requested application form(s)?		
First day to submit?		
Deadline to submit?		
Wrote draft essays/statements for application?		
Essays proofed by at least two other people? Name:_____ Name:_____		
Completed final essays/statements?		
Date submitted college application including the essays/statements and paid application fee?		

College names:		
Date received by college?		
Printed out a copy for your files?		
For your major department		
Downloaded or requested application form for your major department?		
First day to submit?		
Deadline to submit?		
Wrote draft essays/statements for major department?		
Essays proofed by at least two other people? Name:_____ Name:_____		
Completed final essays/statements?		
Submitted department application including the essays/statements?		
Printed out a copy for your files?		
Date received by major department?		
Transcripts		
High schools attended		
High school transcript needed?		
Deadline for receipt?		

College names:		
Date you requested it to be sent?		
Date received by four-year college?		
GED, CHSPE or other high school equivalency needs to be submitted?		
If yes, date you requested it to be sent?		
Date received by college?		
Community colleges attended		
Deadline for receipt of transcripts?		
Community college transcript from current school—name of your school and date you requested it to be sent?		
Date received by four-year college?		
Community college transcripts from other schools—name of each school and date you requested it be sent?		
Date received by four-year college?		
Date sent list of courses in progress to the four-year college?		
Certification (e.g., IGETC) needed by four-year college?		
If yes, date certification sent?		

College names:		
Date received by college?		
Four-year college(s) attended		
Deadline for receipt of transcript(s)?		
Name of four-year college(s) attended and date you requested transcript(s) be sent?		
Date received by transfer four-year college?		
Military transcripts		
Deadline date for receipt of transcript?		
Date received by transfer four-year college?		
Test scores		
Date sent SAT scores (if needed)?		
Date received by college?		
Date sent ACT scores (if needed)?		
Date received by college?		
Date sent AP® scores?		
Date received by college?		
Date sent IB scores?		

College names:		
Date received by college?		
Date sent CLEP scores?		
Date received by college?		
Date sent TOEFL® scores (if needed)?		
Date received by college?		
Letters of recommendation		
Deadline date for receipt?		
Needed for college and major?		
Date requested recommendation #1?		
Date received by college?		
Date requested recommendation #2?		
Date received by college?		
Date requested recommendation #3?		
Date received by college?		
Date requested recommendation #4?		
Date received by college?		
Sent thank you letters to persons giving the recommendations?		
Interviews		
In-person interview required?		

College names:		
If yes, date scheduled and name of interviewer?		
Date completed?		
Telephone interview required?		
If yes, date scheduled and name of interviewer?		
Date completed?		
Sent thank you letters to interviewers?		
Financial aid		
FAFSA deadline date for priority financial aid?		
Deadline date for regular financial aid?		
Date applied for FAFSA?		
Date received FAFSA Student Aid Report showing the EFC (Expected Family Contribution)?		
CSS/Financial Aid PROFILE® needed?		
Priority deadline date for CSS PROFILE?		
Date submitted CSS PROFILE?		
Priority deadline date for state financial aid?		
Date submitted state financial aid form?		
Priority deadline date for the college's financial aid form?		

College names:		
Date submitted college financial aid form?		
Housing application		
Deadline date for priority consideration for housing?		
Date applied for housing?		
Date application received by college?		
Deadline date for required deposit?		
Child care application		
Deadline date for priority consideration?		
Date applied for child care?		
Date application received by college?		
Application status		
College application status?		
Department application status?		
Transcript status?		
Test score: AP/IB/CLEP status?		
Letters of recommendation status?		
Interview status?		

College names:		
Financial aid status?		
Housing status?		
Steps to take when accepted		
Date received admission letter?		
Deadline date to send acceptance of admittance?		
Date received transfer credit report showing articulated and transferable units?		
Date college received your acceptance?		
Deadline date to send deposit?		
Date final transcript sent?		
Date college received final transcript?		
Amount and type of financial aid being offered?		
Date received financial aid award letter?		
Net annual out-of-pocket cost after deducting financial aid?		
Date financial aid award accepted by you?		
Date housing acceptance sent?		

College names:		
Date housing deposit due?		
Date housing deposit sent?		
Date confirmed that housing deposit received?		
Date tuition deposit sent?		
Date confirmed that tuition deposit received?		
Orientation date?		
Signed up for classes?		

Chapter 18

When You're Offered Admission

Congratulations!

When you've been accepted by one or more four-year colleges, you'll need to evaluate the following factors in making a decision:

- Did you get accepted in the major you want?
- How do you feel about the four-year college in general?
- Have you received a transfer credit report that shows how your community college units will transfer to meet lower-division coursework in your major and General Education (GE) requirements as well as elective credit?
- Based on the transfer credit report, how long will it take you to graduate if you take a normal load at the four-year college?
- What scholarships, grants and other financial aid are they offering and will you be able to afford this four-year college?
- Have you already visited the campus?
- Is it a safe campus? Have you looked at the campus security report?
- How large or small is the campus student body?
- How large or small are the classes?
- What are the available housing arrangements and will they work for you?

If you haven't visited the campus before, now is the time to do so. See Chapter 16 on campus visits.

Transfer credit report

If possible, before you agree to attend a four-year college (or turn down other colleges), get a written transfer credit report that shows which courses and units you'll get credit for at the four-year college and how they'll count — toward your major, GE (General Education) requirements, elective credits or no credit at all.

With college so expensive these days, you need to know how many remaining units (and years) you'll be in college. Use the transfer credit report to help you estimate how many more years it will take you to graduate and how much it will cost. Multiply the number of years you'll be at the four-year college by the yearly cost of tuition, fees, books and housing to determine the total cost of your education at a four-year college.

If you feel you've been denied transfer/articulation credit unjustifiably, contact the four-year college and present your case. If that doesn't work, get the community college(s) and four-year college(s) you've attended involved with the transfer issue. Ask what your options are if there is still a problem. Remember: the more units that are accepted, the lower your cost. Don't forget about getting credits through AP, IB and CLEP tests; military service and education; and course substitutions, equivalents and waivers.

Other steps to take once you decide to say yes

- If possible, make sure you have satisfactory housing arrangements *and then* notify the four-year college in writing that you've accepted admission. Most four-year colleges have a formal method of accepting admission. Make sure you follow it.
- Have an official transcript with your final grades sent to the four-year college.

- Contact your faculty advisor in your major at the four-year college as soon as possible.

- Get any other needed academic counseling and go to the earliest available orientation/registration program so you'll have the best chance to sign up for the courses you want. Bring a copy of your transcripts in case your advisors need to reference your courses.

- Make sure you know when tuition, fees, registration and housing payments are due and put them on your calendar.

- Make sure you know the deadlines for adding and dropping courses (put these dates on your calendar) and whether there are a minimum number of units you need to take to stay in college and also to continue to qualify for scholarships and other financial aid.

- Be sure to get tutoring help right away if you need it, especially if you're transferring from a semester system to a quarter system because the pace is so much faster.

What if it doesn't work out at the four-year college?

You may find that you don't want to stay at the four-year college. The motivating factor could be an impossible roommate situation, dissatisfaction with your courses, academic difficulties, financial issues or not connecting on a social level. *Don't give up too quickly.* See whether moving to another room or getting tutoring, counseling, financial or other help will solve the problem.

If you decide you must leave the four-year college, there are three issues to handle:

1. If possible, drop all of your classes before the date you would receive a W (withdrawal) on your academic record.

2. Find out *if* you can get a refund of tuition if you drop all your courses before a certain deadline and make sure you calendar that deadline.

3. Determine the exact procedure for dropping out so you don't inadvertently get W's in your courses or lose your tuition.

Keep in mind you're more likely to really enjoy your four-year college experience if you give it a real "college try." And you just may find these are the best years of your life!

Appendix

All of the websites cited in the book are listed below in the order they appear in a chapter.

Chapter 4
Important Pre-Transfer Issues

California Community Colleges: Finding the Right College
www.cccapply.org/Select/

Chapter 5
Transfer Credit Jargon You Need to Know

Phi Theta Kappa
www.ptk.org

Chapter 8
Step #1: Select the Right Major For You

Choosing a Major
www.washington.edu/uaa/gateway/advising/majors/intro.php

What Can I Do With A Major In
www.uncwil.edu/stuaff/career/Majors/

About.com: What College Majors Will Match Your Personality?
http://homeworktips.about.com/library/maj/bl_majors_quiz.htm

Florida State University Career Center: Matching Majors to Occupations
www.career.fsu.edu/occupations/matchmajor/

Students Review, Inc.: Choosing a Career and Major
www.studentsreview.com/choosing_career.php3

Occupational Outlook Handbook (OOH)
www.bls.gov/oco/

Career Guide to Industries (CGI)
www.bls.gov/OCO/cg/

CareerOneStop: Career Information Net
www.acinet.org/HelpAndInfo.asp?helpcontent=Students&nodeid=102

O*NET Online
http://online.onetcenter.org/

College Board
www.collegeboard.com/student/csearch/majors_careers/index.html

The Princeton Review Online
www.princetonreview.com/default.aspx?uidbadge=%07

University of California—Choose Your Major and Campus
http://uctransfer.universityofcalifornia.edu

Chapter 9
Step #2: Understand Money and Other Big Issues

Federal Student Aid FAFSA4caster
www.fafsa4caster.ed.gov/

Federal Student Aid
www.FederalStudentAid.ed.gov

FinAid EFC Calculator
www.finaid.org/calculators/finaidestimate.phtml

FAFSA
www.fafsa.ed.gov

College Scholarship Service (CSS) Financial Aid Profile®
https://profileonline.collegeboard.com/prf/index.jsp

College Navigator
http://nces.ed.gov/collegenavigator/

Back to College
www.back2college.com

Chapter 10
Step #3: See If There Is a Guaranteed Admission Program

University of Central Florida
www.regionalcampuses.ucf.edu/directconnect.asp

California UC transfer
http://uctransfer.universityofcalifornia.edu/transfer_admis_guar.html

University of California Transfer Admission Guarantee
Program (2009-10) Matrix
http://uctransfer.universityofcalifornia.edu/pdf/tag_matrix_and_form.pdf

Maryland Transfer Advantage Program
www.uga.umd.edu/admissions/apply/MarylandTransferAdvantage.asp

Oregon University System Dual Enrollment Program
www.ous.edu/stucoun/campcent/dual.php

California State University LDTP
www.calstate.edu/acadaff/ldtp
www.calstate.edu/acadaff/ldtp/docs/csu_ccc_mou.pdf

Chapter 11:
Step #4: Assemble a List of Four-Year Colleges to Investigate

Students Review, Inc.
www4.studentsreview.com

College Prowler
http://collegeprowler.com/

College Confidential
www.collegeconfidential.com

Unigo, LLC
www.unigo.com

College Navigator
http://nces.ed.gov/collegenavigator/

The University of Texas at Austin: U.S. Universities: Alphabetic
www.utexas.edu/world/univ/alpha

The University of Texas at Austin: U.S. Universities: By State
www.utexas.edu/world/univ/state

College Board: Find the Right Colleges for You
http://collegesearch.collegeboard.com/search/index.jsp

College Board
www.collegeboard.com

University of Florida: Index of American Universities
www.clas.ufl.edu/au/

The Princeton Review
www.princetonreview.com/default.aspx?uidbadge=%07

Students.gov
www.students.gov

College Directory Network
www.collegedirectorynetwork.com

U.S. News & World Report: Best Colleges 2009
www.usnews.com/usnews/edu/college/rankings/rankindex_brief.php

ASSIST (Articulation System Stimulating Interinstitutional Student Transfer)
www.assist.org

University of California — Choose Your Major and Campus
http://uctransfer.universityofcalifornia.edu

CaliforniaColleges.edu
www.californiacolleges.edu

CSU Mentor
www.csumentor.edu/AboutMentor/mentor.asp

Ohio Board of Regents: Colleges & Universities
http://regents.ohio.gov/colleges_universities.php

College Source
http://collegesource.org

Chapter 12
Step #5: Research the Admission, Transfer and Graduation Requirements

Maryland transfer coordinators
www.mhec.state.md.us/preparing/stuguide.asp#What

New Jersey transfer contacts
www.njtransfer.org/html/contacts.asp?mu=menu_student&mn=contacts&vmode=stude nt

University of Southern California admission counselors
www.usc.edu/admission/undergraduate/prepare/counselor_profiles.html

California Virtual Campus
www.cvc.edu

Chapter 13
Step #6: Ask the Right Questions for You

College Navigator
http://nces.ed.gov/collegenavigator/

RateMyProfessors.com, LLC
www.ratemyprofessors.com

Chapter 14
Step #7: Take the Right Courses

AACRAO (American Association of Collegiate Registrars and Admissions Officers)
www.aacrao.org/pro_development/transfer.cfm

u.select
http://clients.redlanternu.com/home/display/USL/u.select

ASSIST: IGETC (Intersegmental General Education Transfer Curriculum)
www.assist.org/web-assist/help/help-igetc.html

IGETC
www.igetc.org

Arizona aztransfer
www.aztransfer.com/TransferBasics

Illinois Articulation Initiative
www.itransfer.org/container.aspx?file=iai

Florida Department of Education Statewide Course Numbering System
http://scns.fldoe.org/scns/public/pb_index.jsp

Chapter 15
Step #8: Find the Money to Attend a Four-Year College

College Credit for Military Experience
www.military.com/sitemap

AmeriCorps
www.americorps.org

Federal Student Aid FAFSA4caster
www.fafsa4caster.ed.gov/

FinAid Page, LLC
www.finaid.org

College Board
www.collegeboard.com

SallieMae: College Answer
www.collegeanswer.com

FastWeb, LLC
www.fastweb.com

Scholarships.com, LLC
www.scholarships.com

Federal Student Aid
http://studentaid.ed.gov

Phi Theta Kappa
www.ptk.org

California Student Aid Commission: Cal Grants
www.csac.ca.gov/default.asp

Federal Student Aid FAFSA4caster
www.fafsa4caster.ed.gov/

Federal Student Aid
www.FederalStudentAid.ed.gov

FinAid Page, LLC
www.finaid.org/calculators/finaidestimate.phtml

Federal Student Aid FAFSA
www.fafsa.ed.gov

College Scholarship Service (CSS) Financial Aid Profile®
https://profileonline.collegeboard.com/prf/index.jsp

Chapter 16
Step #9: Visit the Campuses

eCampus Tours
www.ecampustours.com

Campus Tours, Inc.
www.campustours.com

YouniversityTV
www.youniversitytv.com

Collegiate Choice Walking Tours DVD Videos
www.collegiatechoice.com

StudentUniverse
www.studentuniverse.com

Campus Visit
www.campusvisit.com

Chapter 17
Step #10: Complete Your Transfer Applications

The Common Application
www.commonapp.org

Educational Testing Service: TOEFL (Test of English as a Foreign Language)
www.ets.org

Glossary

A.A. degree   a two-year degree from a community college, also known as an Associate of Arts degree

A.B. degree   a two-year degree from a community college, also known as an Associate of Business degree (this gets a little confusing because a Bachelor of Arts degree from a four-year college is sometimes referred to as an A.B. degree as well as a B.A. degree)

A.S. degree   a two-year degree from a community college, also known as an Associate of Science degree

accreditation   recognition that a college maintains suitable standards—although not a guarantee of high standards, a lack of accreditation may indicate that other colleges will not accept credits from that college

ACT   an assessment test to assess the general education level of high school students and to determine whether they have the ability to handle college-level work

AP (Advanced Placement)   special courses taken in high school that can allow students to get college credit

articulated course   a course that is determined to be an equivalent course at another college and/or a course that by itself or in combination with one or more courses satisfies a General Education and/or lower-division major requirement

articulation agreement   an agreement between colleges that identifies equivalent courses and gives transferring students credit for courses taken at one of the colleges

Associate of Arts degree (*see* A.A. degree)

Associate of Business degree (*see* A.B. degree)

Associate of Science degree (*see* A.S. degree)

bachelor's degree   a degree from a four-year college or university either as a B.A. (bachelor of arts) or a B.S. (bachelor of science)

CHSPE   The California High School Proficiency Exam, similar to a GED, is a special exam that provides a certificate in lieu of completing high school (and *may* be considered an equivalent to a high school diploma)

CLEP (College-Level Examination Program®)   a testing program that may earn you college credits

Co-admission (*see* dual enrollment)

College-Level Examination Program® (*see* CLEP)

Common Application   a college admission application used by over 360 colleges—colleges may use it as the sole application or with a supplemental application

community college   also known as junior college, it is a two-year college with academic and vocational programs

core curriculum (*see* General Education requirements)

CSS PROFILE   also known as the CSS/Financial Aid PROFILE®, it is a financial aid form used by some colleges and universities for awarding financial aid

dual enrollment   a program where a student right out of high school is admitted to both a community college and a four-year college

EFC (*see* expected family contribution)

Expected Family Contribution (EFC)   the amount the federal government determines via the FAFSA that students and their families should pay toward college costs

FAFSA   the Free Application for Federal Student Aid form required to receive federal student aid (*www.fafsa.ed.gov*)

GE courses *See* General Education requirements

GED (General Educational Development)   a series of tests to receive a high school equivalency certificate in lieu of a high school diploma

General Education requirements   also known as GE courses, these are courses in English, math, the arts and natural/social sciences that are required for graduation from a four-year college

IB (*see* International Baccalaureate)

IGETC   a transfer core curriculum that fulfills the lower division General Education requirements of both the UC (University of California) and CSU (California State University) systems

International Baccalaureate   Worldwide programs of international education (*www.ibo.org*) that may provide college credit through HL (High Level) tests

LDTP   California State University program with two components: (1) a statewide component giving students a road map for General Education *and* lower-division major courses that have statewide acceptance and (2) a campus component giving the highest priority for admission to a specific campus and major (subject to enrollment demand, available space and satisfactory completion of the requirements in the LDTP contract).

lower division   the first two years of college (freshman and sophomore years)

Lower Division Transfer Patterns *See* LDTP

priority deadline   a deadline for financial aid, admission, housing and/or child care that gives you priority consideration if you meet the deadline

rolling admission   a system allowing transfer students to apply throughout the school year and possibly summer, too, for admission to a four-year college

TAA *See* transfer admission agreement

TAG *See* transfer admission guarantee

TAP *See* transfer advantage program

TOEFL   an English as a foreign language proficiency exam for college

transfer admission agreement (TAA) *See* transfer admission guarantee

transfer admission guarantee   program that may be available in your state that guarantees admission to certain four-year colleges if you sign a transfer admission guarantee (TAG) or a transfer admission agreement (TAA) contract, complete the specified coursework at certain community colleges in that state and maintain a specified minimum GPA

transfer advantage program   program that may be available in your state that guarantees admission to certain four-year colleges if you sign a transfer advantage program (TAP) agreement, complete the specified coursework at certain community colleges in that state and maintain a specified minimum GPA

transfer coordinator   a counselor at a community college and/or a four-year college that helps transfer students at a community college select the right courses, provides information on course and/or program transferability and assists students who want to appeal a denial of transfer credit

transfer guide   a brochure or other document spelling out the do's and don'ts to transfer from a community college to a particular four-year college

transfer counselor (*see* transfer coordinator)

transferable course a course that gets credit at a four-year college as a general education and/or lower-division major course or as an elective course

transfer credit report   a written document from a four-year college showing how many community college units will receive credit for General Education courses, lower-division major courses and elective courses.

transfer director (*see* transfer coordinator)

upper division   the last two years of college (junior and senior years)

Author Bio

Don Silver

Dr. Don Silver is an educational consultant for *The Wall Street Journal Classroom Edition Teacher Guide* and has taught at USC. Both his undergraduate and doctoral degrees are from UCLA. He is the author of 12 highly acclaimed books. Dr. Silver also has personal and practical experience with the transfer process as a father. Dr. Silver's son was accepted at every university he applied to as a transfer student including one program that accepts only four percent of applicants.

Dr. Silver's books are used in schools, colleges and universities across the nation to teach personal finance, business ethics and law. Among his books are *High School Money Book*, *A Parent's Guide to Wills &* Trusts, *Teach Your Computer to Dance*, *Cookin' the Book$* and *Baby Boomer Retirement*.

Dr. Silver is most proud that he is the father of a wonderful son, who three months after his 17th birthday, transferred from a community college to a major university with over a year's worth of college credits. Dr. Silver and his son also discovered firsthand the many challenges of making this transfer.

In this book Dr. Silver hopes to make the complex and often-confusing path from community college to a four-year college or university a lot smoother, more understandable and less costly.

Index